To:

_____

From:

_____

about the author

Bestselling author Karol Ladd offers lasting hope and biblical truth to women around the world through her Positive book series. A gifted communicator and dynamic leader, Karol is founder and president of Positive Life Principles, Inc., a resource company offering strategies for success in both home and work. Her vivacious personality makes her a popular speaker for women's organizations, church groups, and corporate events. She is cofounder of a character-building club for young girls called USA Sonshine Girls and serves on several educational boards. Karol is a frequent guest on radio and television programs. Her most valued role is that of wife to Curt and mother to daughters Grace and Joy. Visit her website at PositiveLifePrinciples.com.

the
power of a
positive
wife

Devotional & Journal

52 Monday Morning Motivations

Karol Ladd

HOWARD BOOKS
A DIVISION OF SIMON & SCHUSTER
New York   London   Toronto   Sydney

Our purpose at Howard Books is to:
- *Increase faith* in the hearts of growing Christians
- *Inspire holiness* in the lives of believers
- *Instill hope* in the hearts of struggling people everywhere
  Because He's coming again!

 Published by Howard Books, a division of Simon & Schuster, Inc.
1230 Avenue of the Americas, New York, NY 10020
www.howardpublishing.com

The Power of a Positive Wife Devotional & Journal © 2008 by Karol Ladd

Published in association with the Steve Laube Agency

Library of Congress Cataloging-in-Publication Data
Ladd, Karol.
The power of a positive wife devotional & journal: 52 Monday morning motivations /
Karol Ladd.
p. cm.
1. Wives—Religious life. 2. Spiritual journals—Authorship. I. Title.
BV4528.15.L333 2008
242'.6435—dc22
2008009120

ISBN-13: 978-1-4165-7902-1
ISBN-10:   1-4165-7902-8

1 3 5 7 9 10 8 6 4 2
HOWARD and colophon are registered trademarks of Simon & Schuster, Inc.

Manufactured in the United States of America

For information regarding special discounts for bulk purchases, please contact:
Simon & Schuster Special Sales at 1-800-456-6798 or business@simonandschuster.com.

Edited by Michelle Buckingham

Copyright notice continues on page 213.

contents

contents

introduction

*I*t has been said that marriage is made in heaven—but it still takes a lot of work down here on earth! Let's be honest: marriage requires a great deal of intentional effort. If you're like me, you desire a strong and fulfilling relationship with your husband. You want an ever-deepening bond of love to grow between the two of you. That's the goal of every positive wife. But what does it take? What is the key to building an intimate and lasting connection with the man you married?

The answer may surprise you: as you grow deeper in a love relationship with God, your relationship with your husband will be greatly enhanced. How can I make such a bold statement? Because when a woman finds her sufficiency, strength, and hope in Christ, she tends to relate well with the people around her, especially her spouse.

In my own marriage, I have come to recognize that as I draw close to Christ, one of the beautiful benefits is the wisdom, love, and confidence I increasingly have in my relationship with my husband, Curt. I've also noticed that the opposite is true: when I center my hopes and expectations in my husband, I find myself in a place of unrest in my relationship with him.

As wives, we may be tempted to look to our husbands for fulfillment and joy instead of to the Lord. As a result, we develop an unhealthy dependence on our husbands to meet all of our needs, and our marriages can suffer. If we put our faith and trust in God first, however, we strike a much healthier balance and put our marriages on the track to success.

Here's what I've discovered: as we walk intimately with the God who loves us with an unfailing love, we learn how to sincerely love others. As we relish the fact that we are completely forgiven through Christ, we become more forgiving people. As we see God's powerful hand at work, we live in the confident assurance that God is with us and has a plan for us. And as we recognize the redemption that God brings, we embrace the living hope that God can and will transform our marriages.

The purpose of this devotional book is lofty, I admit. My goal is to draw you into a deeper, more intimate love relationship with God through reflection, prayer, and time spent in his Word. My hope and desire is that your marriage will be enhanced, blessed, and strengthened in the process.

Inside you will find fifty-two Monday Morning Motivations, one for each week of the year. The idea is for you to set aside time on Monday mornings for each week's devotional. What a great way to start your week! But if Monday mornings aren't good for you, choose another day or time. Just be consistent. Each devotional includes a passage of Scripture and a reflection for you to apply to your life, with a focus on your role as a positive wife. The Scripture passages have the unique feature of taking you all the way through the Bible, starting in Genesis in week 1 and ending in Revelation in week 52.

This is an interactive book. By all means, write in it! I have provided space for you to record your answers to the thought-provoking questions raised in each week's study. I've also left room for you to record any positive choices you want to make in active response to what you've learned. In addition, I have written a sample prayer for each devotional to help guide you in your own prayer life, followed by enough space for you to write down your prayer requests for the week ahead.

One feature I am especially excited about is the Couple's Discussion Starter. As you reflect on a specific devotional through the week, I encourage you to use the Discussion Starter to open up a conversation with your husband about your marriage relationship and about your relationship as a couple with God. My prayer is that these discussions will help to build and enhance the spiritual bond between you.

As I wrote this book and prayerfully progressed through each passage of Scripture, I began to recognize one underlying theme. Over and over again I saw the mighty hand of God at work. I saw his power to revolutionize our lives and our marriages. In every book in the Bible, I saw a powerful and loving God who desires for his people to come to him. Often, as wives, we try to solve our marital problems or fix our husbands in our own way. But God wants us to come to him first and seek his wisdom, power, and help.

My sincere prayer is that in the weeks and months ahead you will come to know (for the first time, or all over again) that God loves you, and you will choose to draw near to him. There is joy and delight in the safety of his arms! Make a decision today to be a positive wife who puts her faith and trust in God. I guarantee that you will be transformed—and so will your marriage.

the

power of a
positive
wife

Devotional & Journal

Week 1

Two United as One

📖 **Key Scripture:** Genesis 2:18, 22–24

The Lord God said, "It is not good for the man to be alone. I will make a companion who will help him. . . ." Then the Lord God made a woman from the rib and brought her to Adam.

"At last!" Adam exclaimed. "She is part of my own flesh and bone! She will be called 'woman,' because she was taken out of a man." This explains why a man leaves his father and mother and is joined to his wife, and the two are united into one.

A single man has not nearly the value he would have in the state of union. He is an incomplete animal. He resembles the odd half of a pair of scissors.

—Benjamin Franklin

❀ Reflection

What a beautiful, divine concept—two people becoming one flesh! But what's the point? Why did God create the institution of marriage? Wouldn't it be easier if we all just lived happily on our own (no arguments or annoyances or frustrations)? Our passage today gives us the answer. "It is not good for the man to be alone."

As wives, we help our husbands; we are a gift to them. Do you see yourself as a gift to your husband? Your words of encouragement can strengthen him, your acts of loving-kindness can support him, and your gifts and personality can work together with his to create an amazing team. Without you, he is incomplete. Together, you are a family unit. Society is built on the foundation of healthy marriages, and you and your husband help to give it a firm footing.

Of course, when two imperfect people come together, there will be struggle. As two lives are meshed into one, there will be times of conflict and strife. Yet from the blending of two individuals comes the beauty of the marriage bond. When you and your husband got married, you didn't lose your autonomy; rather, you came together as two separate people whose gifts, talents, and personalities strengthen and complete each other. You and your husband are a team, designed by God to work together as one flesh and enrich the community in which you live.

⊚ My Thoughts

What does it mean to be "united into one?" Am I struggling against being one flesh, or am I working toward it?

_____

_____

_____

_____

_____

♡ My Prayer

Glorious Father, creator of all things, I praise you for your love for mankind. Thank you for the institution of marriage. Thank you for your divine plan of putting one man and one woman together so the two may become one flesh. Help my husband and me to grow together. Mold us and fashion us to complement each other. Give us wisdom to work through our differences and build on our strengths. In Jesus' name I pray, amen.

This week I am praying for: _____

_____

_____

_____

_____

_____

_____

☀ My Choices

* This week I will choose to look for ways to encourage and complete my husband.

* This week I will choose to support my husband through prayer.

* This week I will choose to look for ways God can use my unique gifts and talents in my marriage.

* This week I will choose to: _____

_____

_____

_____

_____

◊ Couple's Discussion Starter

In what specific ways do we complete each other?

📖 For Further Reading: GENESIS 1–3

Marriages are made in Heaven.

—ALFRED, LORD TENNYSON

Week 2

Not So Fast!

📖 **Key Scripture:** EXODUS 13:17–18

When Pharaoh finally let the people go, God did not lead them on the road that runs through Philistine territory, even though that was the shortest way from Egypt to the Promised Land. God said, "If the people are faced with a battle, they might change their minds and return to Egypt." So God led them along a route through the wilderness toward the Red Sea, and the Israelites left Egypt like a marching army.

Second only to suffering, waiting may be the greatest teacher and trainer in godliness, maturity, and genuine spirituality most of us ever encounter.

—RICHARD HENDRIX

 Reflection

Hooray! The Israelites had just been freed from slavery in Egypt, and now God was lovingly leading them to the Promised Land—but in a very roundabout way. If I had been in charge, I would have led the Israelites on the most direct route from Point A (Egyptian slavery) to Point B (Promised Land). I guess it is a good thing I'm not in charge! God chose *not* to lead his precious people along the shortest route. He had their safety and best interests in mind, so he led them on a circuitous journey through the wilderness toward the Red Sea.

The fact is, the shortest route isn't always the best route. In our hurry-up world, we tend to want results immediately. But God may have a better plan—a more powerful plan.

You may feel as if you are in the wilderness in your marriage or your circumstances, and you want the situation fixed *now*! Dear friend, I encourage you to prayerfully wait upon the Lord. The same God who parted the Red Sea for the Israelites is at work in our lives. He has a greater purpose and plan than our own. As you and I learn to trust God through our personal valleys and wilderness experiences, our character is developed and our faith grows. We may not understand why he is taking us along a certain route—but we can always trust his love for us.

⊚ My Thoughts

Are there areas in my life where I am frustrated because I am not seeing immediate results? Am I able to give those areas over to the Lord and wait patiently for him? _____

_____

_____

_____

♡ My Prayer

Wonderful and all-wise heavenly Father, I praise you, for you do all things well! Even when I don't understand your ways, I trust your loving care for me. Thank you for not always taking me down the easiest or quickest road on my life's journey. I trust that you know what is best for me. I believe that you are always with me, in the good times and in the trials. Help me to remember that the power you showed when you parted the Red Sea is available to help me overcome whatever seems impossible in my life. Be my strength in my wilderness journey. I rejoice in you! In Jesus' name, amen.

This week I am praying for: _____

_____

_____

_____

_____

_____

☼ My Choices

* This week I will choose to prayerfully wait on God.

* This week I will choose to trust God's loving power in my life, even when I don't understand why I am going through the wilderness.

* This week I will choose to find joy in the journey and not just the destination.

* This week I will choose to: _____

_____

_____

_____

_____

◊ Couple's Discussion Starter

In what ways have we seen God's loving hand at work through the wildernesses and detours of our life together?

📖 For Further Reading: EXODUS 13–15

Not enjoyment, and not sorrow,
Is our destined end or way,
But to act, that each to-morrow,
Find us farther than to-day.

—HENRY WADSWORTH LONGFELLOW

Week 3

His Very Own

📖 Key Scripture: LEVITICUS 20:24, 26

*I have promised that you will inherit their land, a land
flowing with milk and honey. I, the LORD, am your God,
who has set you apart from all other people. . . . You must
be holy because I, the LORD, am holy. I have set you apart
from all other people to be my very own.*

The serene beauty of a holy life
is the most powerful influence in the world
next to the power of God.

—BLAISE PASCAL

 # Reflection

The book of Leviticus centers on holiness. The word *holy* means "set apart." God desires for his people to be set apart—but why? So he can be difficult and place a heavy burden on those he calls his own? No, quite the contrary. God is holy *and* loving. As a loving God, he wants the best for his people. The Levitical offerings God required of the Israelites allowed an unholy people to draw near to a holy God through sacrificial atonement and receive forgiveness. Also, many of the Levitical laws served to keep the people clean and safe from diseases that were common in that day.

It's easy to get bogged down in all the rules as you read Leviticus, but let's look at it through the eyes of love. A holy God chooses to reach down and draw unholy people close to himself. We learn of God's desire for us to live a holy and righteous life in the pages of Leviticus, yet in the New Testament we see the completion of his divine plan. God loved the world so much that he sent the once-and-for-all sacrifice, his Son, Jesus, as the Lamb of God who takes away our sin. He makes us holy and forgiven through faith in Jesus. Yes, God is perfectly holy—and abounding in perfect love!

⊚ My Thoughts

How does God's love toward me and his desire for my holiness affect my obedience to him? _____

_____

_____

_____

_____

♡ My Prayer

Most holy Father, it is amazing to think that you care about me and want to have a relationship with me! I praise you for your perfect love and holiness. Thank you for providing a way for me to approach you through your Son, Jesus. I am so grateful that Jesus gave his life on the cross as the final sacrifice, and I can stand in a place of forgiveness and grace because of what he has done. Help me to live a life pleasing to you. Convict me of sin and lead me away from temptation, so that I may bring glory to you through holy living. In Jesus' name I pray, amen.

This week I am praying for: _____

_____

_____

_____

_____

_____

_____

☀ My Choices

* This week I will choose to reflect on God's holiness.

* This week I will choose to examine areas in my life that are not pleasing to him.

* This week I will choose to seek God's help in turning from sin.

* This week I will choose to: _____

_____

_____

_____

_____

✒ Couple's Discussion Starter

Why does our society use the term "holy matrimony"? In what ways does our relationship reflect holiness?

📖 For Further Reading: LEVITICUS 26

The New Testament does not say that Christians must lead holy lives in order to become saints; instead, it tells Christians that, because they are saints, they must henceforth lead holy lives!

—J. I. PACKER

Week 4

Eyes of Faith

📖 Key Scripture: NUMBERS 14:5–9

Moses and Aaron fell face down on the ground before the people of Israel. Two of the men who had explored the land, Joshua son of Nun and Caleb son of Jephunneh, tore their clothing. They said to the community of Israel, "The land we explored is a wonderful land! And if the LORD is pleased with us, he will bring us safely into that land and give it to us. It is a rich land flowing with milk and honey, and he will give it to us! Do not rebel against the LORD, and don't be afraid of the people of the land. They are only helpless prey to us! They have no protection, but the LORD is with us! Don't be afraid of them!"

We look with an eye of faith farther
than we can see with an eye of sense.

—MATTHEW HENRY

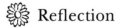 Reflection

Twelve Israelite spies returned to give their report of the Promised Land. Ten said, "No!" Two said, "Go!" Only two had eyes of faith. Caleb and Joshua focused on the bountiful blessings of the land. The other ten were so focused on the giants that they couldn't see the beauty of what God was giving them. They forgot the "God factor." Remember our passage from last week? God told the Israelites he would give them the land—and he had the power to make it happen.

How does this story apply to us? It's easy to be like the ten spies and focus on the giant negatives in our lives and in our husbands. How often do we lose faith in God's power to do a mighty work beyond what we can see? As positive wives, we need to turn our eyes toward faith in what God can do and stop concentrating on what's wrong. Look at what's promising, not what's discouraging! By changing your focus, you will begin to see all the positive blessings God has provided—and will provide—in the Promised Land of your marriage.

⊙ My Thoughts

In what areas am I concentrating on the negatives, when I should be looking for the positive possibilities? _____

_____

_____

_____

_____

_____

_____

♡ My Prayer

Magnificent Lord, I praise you, because you can be trusted. You are faithful and true. You will never leave me. Thank you for being very real to me in my life. Lord, I want to keep my eyes on you. Increase my faith. Keep me from doubt. Help me to focus on what you can do beyond what I see in front of me. You are able to do all things! I believe; help my unbelief. In Jesus' name, amen.

This week I am praying for: _____

_____

_____

_____

_____

_____

_____

_____

☼ My Choices

* This week I will choose to recognize areas of my life where I am concentrating on the negatives.

* This week I will choose to replace those negative thoughts with faith-filled thoughts.

* This week I will choose to see the possibilities in the people around me—especially my husband.

* This week I will choose to: _____

_____

_____

_____

_____

✎ Couple's Discussion Starter

What positive blessings can we be grateful for in our marriage?

📖 For Further Reading: NUMBERS 13–14

Faith does the same against the devil
as unbelief does against God.

—JOHN BUNYAN

Week 5

Objects of His Love

📖 **Key Scripture:** DEUTERONOMY 10:12–16

"And now, Israel, what does the LORD your God require of you? He requires you to fear him, to live according to his will, to love and worship him with all your heart and soul, and to obey the LORD's commands and laws that I am giving you today for your own good. The highest heavens and the earth and everything in it all belong to the LORD your God. Yet the LORD chose your ancestors as the objects of his love. And he chose you, their descendants, above every other nation, as is evident today. Therefore, cleanse your sinful hearts and stop being stubborn."

God loves us the way we are,
but he loves us too much to leave us that way.

—LEIGHTON FORD

 # Reflection

Moses addressed the Israelites with a powerful charge: fear the Lord, live in a way that pleases him, love him, and serve him. But he didn't just give them the command; he also gave them two motivations. He told them that obeying God was for their own good, and he reminded them that God chose them as the objects of his love.

"The objects of God's love." Hold on to that statement for a moment and reflect on it. As followers of Christ, we, too, are a part of God's family and the objects of his love. His love satisfies the longing in our souls. It draws us closer to him and makes us want to love him, serve him, and walk in obedience to his Word.

Dear sister in Christ, there may be days when you don't feel so loveable to others; but remember, you are the object of God's love! Sincere and pure love is a motivating factor in any relationship. Did you notice the last statement in our passage today? "Cleanse your sinful hearts and stop being stubborn." Are you being stubborn in some way in your relationship with God? What about in your relationship with your husband? Because you are deeply loved by God, cleanse your heart—and see how selfless love can make a relationship blossom and grow.

 My Thoughts

Are there any areas of stubbornness in my heart that I
need to deal with? _____

_____

_____

_____

_____

_____

♡ My Prayer

Loving and gracious heavenly Father, I thank you for allowing me to be an object of your love! It is wonderful to
be loved and cared for by you. Lord, help me to live in
obedience to you. Help me to love you sincerely and serve
you faithfully. My desire is to honor and please you in my
marriage and every aspect of my life. Cleanse my heart
and turn me away from my stubborn tendencies. In Jesus'
name I pray, amen.

This week I am praying for: _____

_____

_____

_____

_____

_____

_____

_____

☼ My Choices

* This week I will choose to reflect on the beauty of being an object of God's love.

* This week I will choose to examine ways in which I may be stubborn.

* This week I will choose to obey God because of his love for me.

* This week I will choose to: _____

_____

_____

_____

_____

◐ Couple's Discussion Starter

As objects of God's love, how can we as a couple live a life that is pleasing to God?

📖 For Further Reading: DEUTERONOMY 8–11

If a man could know that he was loved of all his fellow men, if he could have it for certain that he was loved by all the angels, . . . yet these were but so many drops and all put together could not compare with the main ocean contained in the fact that "God loved us."

—CHARLES H. SPURGEON

Week 6

God's Transforming Work

📖 **Key Scripture:** JOSHUA 2:8–13

Before the spies went to sleep that night, Rahab went up on the roof to talk with them. "I know the LORD has given you this land," she told them. "We are all afraid of you. Everyone is living in terror. For we have heard how the LORD made a dry path for you through the Red Sea when you left Egypt. And we know what you did to Sihon and Og, the two Amorite kings east of the Jordan River, whose people you completely destroyed. No wonder our hearts have melted in fear! No one has the courage to fight after hearing such things. For the LORD your God is the supreme God of the heavens above and the earth below. Now swear to me by the LORD that you will be kind to me and my family since I have helped you. Give me some guarantee that when Jericho is conquered, you will let me live, along with my father and mother, my brothers and sisters, and all their families."

 Reflection

In our reading today, Rahab made an amazing and powerful statement of faith. Although she was not an Israelite, she knew that the Israelite God was God. She believed, and she acted on her belief. Her faith made a difference in her life. But Rahab was no sweet little angel; she was the local prostitute of Jericho! God reached down and touched the heart of a sinful woman and used her in a mighty way.

Rahab's story is much like every Christian's story. God didn't save us and choose to use us because we were perfect women. Quite the contrary; the New Testament says, "While we were still sinners, Christ died for us" (Romans 5:8 NIV). Just as Rahab's faith brought her salvation, so we are made righteous through our faith in Christ. Our faith transforms our lives, just as Rahab's faith transformed hers.

Rahab went on to marry an Israelite named Salmon, and her name is forever listed in the lineage of Jesus. Aren't you thankful that God takes sinners and transforms their lives through faith?

⊚ My Thoughts

How has Christ's transforming work in me made a difference in the things I say and do and the way I live my life?

_____

_____

_____

_____

_____

♡ My Prayer

Wonderful, glorious, gracious Father, thank you for sending your Son, Jesus, to die for sinners like me. Thank you for the transforming power of faith in Christ. Help me to honor you with my life. Do a great work in me and through me, so that others may come to faith in Jesus. Thank you for the example of Rahab, whose life was transformed through faith. Allow me to see the potential in the people around me, trusting your transforming power in their lives. In Jesus' name I pray, amen.

This week I am praying for: _____

_____

_____

_____

_____

_____

☼ My Choices

- ⋆ This week I will choose to thank God for redeeming a sinner like me.

- ⋆ This week I will choose to remember that with God, all things are possible.

- ⋆ This week I will choose to love the sinner, not the sin, as I interact with the people around me.

- ⋆ This week I will choose to: _____

_____
_____
_____
_____

◖ Couple's Discussion Starter

How does our faith in Christ change the way we relate to each other?

📖 For Further Reading: JOSHUA 2–6

Faith is knowledge passing into conviction,
and it is conviction passing into confidence.

—JOHN MURRAY

Week 7

The Power to Manipulate

📖 **Key Scripture:** Judges 16:15–17

Then Delilah pouted, "How can you say you love me when you don't confide in me? You've made fun of me three times now, and you still haven't told me what makes you so strong!" So day after day she nagged him until he couldn't stand it any longer.

Finally, Samson told her his secret. "My hair has never been cut," he confessed, "for I was dedicated to God as a Nazirite from birth. If my head were shaved, my strength would leave me, and I would become as weak as anyone else."

If you wish to enrich days, plant flowers; if you wish to enrich years, plant trees; if you wish to enrich Eternity, plant ideals in the lives of others.

—S. Truett Cathy

 Reflection

You are probably already familiar with the story of Samson and Delilah. Delilah was in cahoots with the Philistines, and she used her power of manipulation to persuade Samson to reveal the secret of his strength. Her deception led to the downfall of a great leader of Israel.

Let's face it: as wives, we can influence our husbands in a powerful way. The question is, are we using our influence for good purposes or for selfish ones? Notice that Delilah used the tactics of pouting, nagging, and deception to manipulate Samson. Her motive was not Samson's best interest, but her own gain. What tactics do you use to influence your husband? As positive wives, we want to steer clear of negative forms of manipulation, such as pouting, whining, nagging, and dishonesty. Instead, through sincerity, encouragement, and loving-kindness, we want to motivate and inspire our husbands to be all God created them to be.

Let's be careful and wise in the way we use our influence and power in our husbands' lives. Let's choose not to manipulate, but to pray—and leave the greater work and results to God.

◎ My Thoughts

What is my motivation when I try to influence or manipulate my husband's actions or decisions? _____

_____

_____

_____

_____

_____

♥ My Prayer

Mighty Lord, I praise you for your great power to change lives. You alone are the one who deals with people's hearts. Forgive me for the times I have tried to manipulate my husband for my own gain or personal desires. Reveal to me my wrong motives, and help me to be a positive influence in my husband's life. Bless the communication in our marriage. May it always be pleasing to you! Do a powerful work in my husband's life—and in mine. In Jesus' name I pray, amen.

This week I am praying for: _____

_____

_____

_____

_____

_____

_____

☀ My Choices

* This week I will choose to identify any forms of manipulation I use in my relationships with others.

* This week I will choose to pray for my husband and trust God to work in his life.

* This week I will choose to look for ways my husband and I can work together as a couple.

* This week I will choose to: _____

_____
_____
_____
_____

✎ Couple's Discussion Starter

What are some of the ways we motivate and influence each other to be our best? Are there any forms of manipulation that need to be stopped?

📖 For Further Reading: JUDGES 13–16

There is no end to the influence of women on our life.
It is at the bottom of everything that happens to us.

—BENJAMIN DISRAELI

Week 8

Beauty from Ashes

📖 Key Scripture: RUTH 1:19–22

The two of them continued on their journey. When they came to Bethlehem, the entire town was stirred by their arrival. "Is it really Naomi?" the women asked.

"Don't call me Naomi," she told them. "Instead, call me Mara, for the Almighty has made life very bitter for me. I went away full, but the LORD has brought me home empty. Why should you call me Naomi when the LORD has caused me to suffer and the Almighty has sent such tragedy?"

So Naomi returned from Moab, accompanied by her daughter-in-law Ruth, the young Moabite woman. They arrived in Bethlehem at the beginning of the barley harvest.

Hope is the only tie
which keeps the heart from breaking.

—THOMAS FULLER

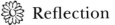 Reflection

Ruth and Naomi were walking a difficult road together, returning to Naomi's homeland after suffering great loss. Naomi lost not only her husband but also her two sons. Her daughter-in-law, Ruth, chose to stay with her in a beautiful demonstration of love and loyalty to Naomi and to God. When they arrived in Bethlehem, Naomi was very honest with her friends about her pain. She told them to no longer call her Naomi, which means "pleasant," but rather Mara, which means "bitter."

Certainly Naomi needed to grieve and mourn. She was honest about her suffering, even with God. The good news is that God had not left her. In the midst of her pain, he provided. Ruth was a gift from God to Naomi, and through Ruth's loyalty, God created a beautiful new life from the ashes of pain and bitterness. Eventually Ruth married an Israelite named Boaz, and they had a son. The women of the town rejoiced with Naomi, saying, "Praise the LORD who has given you a family redeemer today!" (Ruth 4:14). Little did they know that God had, in fact, given much more. Ruth and Boaz went on to be the great-grandparents of King David, in the direct lineage of the great Redeemer, Jesus!

Perhaps you've felt bitter like Naomi. Certainly, there is a time to cry and grieve and be honest about our pain. As positive wives, however, we must not wallow in bitterness. We must move past it, trusting God to bring beauty and blessing from even the most difficult circumstances. Our God is a redeeming God! Let's turn our eyes toward the hope he provides.

⊚ My Thoughts

Am I holding on to any bitterness or resentment in my heart? Am I willing to give the circumstances over to God and release the bitterness? _____

_____

_____

_____

♡ My Prayer

Redeeming God, I praise you, because you make all things new. You resurrect the dead, heal the sick, and transform lives. You bring good even from dismal situations. Turn my eyes toward the hope that you bring! Help me to honestly work through my feelings of anger, bitterness, and grief, and then give me the strength to move on. Thank you for your provision, even when I don't deserve it. You are faithful, loving, and kind! In Jesus' name I pray, amen.

This week I am praying for: _____

_____

_____

_____

_____

_____

☼ My Choices

* This week I will choose to be honest about my pain and hurt.

* This week I will choose to look for hope in every situation.

* This week I will choose to let go of my bitterness and grief and trust God's care for me.

* This week I will choose to: _____

_____

_____

_____

_____

✒ Couple's Discussion Starter

How has God brought hope and redemption to the sad painful, or difficult times in our lives?

📖 For Further Reading: THE BOOK OF RUTH

Hope, like the gleaming taper's light,
Adorns and cheers our way;
And still, as darker grows the night,
Emits a brighter ray.

—OLIVER GOLDSMITH

Week 9

Surefootedness

📖 Key Scripture: 2 SAMUEL 22:31–37

As for God, his way is perfect.
All the LORD's promises prove true.
He is a shield for all who look to him for protection.
For who is God except the LORD?
Who but our God is a solid rock?
God is my strong fortress;
he has made my way safe.
He makes me as surefooted as a deer,
leading me safely along the mountain heights.
He prepares me for battle;
he strengthens me to draw a bow of bronze.
You have given me the shield of your salvation;
your help has made me great.
You have made a wide path for my feet
to keep them from slipping.

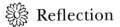 Reflection

Have you ever felt in over your head in a situation? Maybe it was an obligation at work or an overloaded schedule at home. Maybe you were counseling a troubled friend or dealing with a rough spot in your marriage. David's song reminds us that God is able to lead and guide us through even the most difficult situations. David declared that God had given him feet like a deer; he was able to climb difficult mountains in life because God was with him.

David's life was no cakewalk. It was filled with battles and death threats and rebellious children. But through these challenges, he learned to trust God's provision. Notice all the wonderful ways David saw God at work: God prepared him for battle; God strengthened him; God gave him the shield of salvation; God made his way safe. David had stepped out in faith on many occasions, and God had provided. Now, when David looked back over his life, he couldn't help but praise the Lord!

What about you? Do you see God as your strong fortress and your help? Are you willing to follow him in the direction he leads you, knowing that his ways are perfect and he will make a wide path for your feet? We can have confidence that God will give us the feet we need for the journey ahead, whether it is a smooth path or a rocky road. May we be like David and sing God's praises as he leads us, protects us, and carries us through life.

⊚ My Thoughts

Do I try to make it through difficulties in my own strength, or do I look to God as my help and provider? _____

_____

_____

_____

_____

_____

♡ My Prayer

Dear Father, I praise you, for you are my protector and provider. You are a strong tower; I run to you and find refuge. Thank you for hearing my prayers. Thank you for giving me everything I need for the journey ahead. Help me to keep my eyes continually on you, and teach me to trust in your strength instead of my own. Keep my feet from stumbling, and lead me along your perfect path. In Jesus' name, amen.

This week I am praying for: _____

_____

_____

_____

_____

_____

_____

☀ My Choices

* This week I will choose to see God as my refuge and strength.

* This week I will choose to turn over my challenges to him and seek his leading.

* This week I will choose to praise him for his care and provision for me.

* This week I will choose to: _____

_____

_____

_____

_____

◗ Couple's Discussion Starter

Have there been times in our lives when we've felt overwhelmed and in need of God's help? How did God provide?

📖 For Further Reading: 2 SAMUEL 22–23

We must learn to cease from measuring the power of God by our own, and reasoning from one to the other.

—MARCUS DODS

Week 10

Forgotten Blessings, Worthless Idols

📖 **Key Scripture:** 2 KINGS 17:13–15

Again and again the LORD had sent his prophets and seers to warn both Israel and Judah: "Turn from all your evil ways. Obey my commands and laws, which are contained in the whole law that I commanded your ancestors and which I gave you through my servants the prophets."

But the Israelites would not listen. They were as stubborn as their ancestors and refused to believe in the LORD their God. They rejected his laws and the covenant he had made with their ancestors, and they despised all his warnings. They worshiped worthless idols and became worthless themselves. They followed the example of the nations around them, disobeying the LORD's command not to imitate them.

An idol may be defined as any person or thing that has usurped in the heart the place of preeminence that belongs to the Lord.

—ARTHUR WALLIS

Reflection

God loves his people and is patient with them. He tenderly calls them back to himself. In our passage today, we have a picture of God's precious people, the Israelites, in a state of forgetfulness. They had forgotten all the wonderful blessings that God had provided for them and their ancestors before them. God miraculously delivered them from slavery in Egypt, victoriously led them through the wilderness, and generously gave them the Promised Land. Yet it was in this wonderful land that the Israelites began to turn their eyes away from God and toward the idols of the nations around them.

It is so easy for us to look at this picture of stubbornness and disobedience and say, "How could these people turn from their loving God?" But the picture hasn't really changed much. How often do you and I shift from loving God with all our hearts and minds to loving "stuff" with all our hearts and minds? Whether we are consumed with home decorating or fashion or making money, worthless idols can often take the place of God in our lives.

Sometimes our idols aren't "stuff" but things like security or orderliness or even ourselves. Husbands can become idols, too. As positive wives, we must be careful not to make our husbands into idols, thinking that a man can meet all of our needs. Let's ask God to help us become aware of any idols we tend to place on the thrones of our hearts. Just as he alerted the Israelites, he can alert us. He stands with his arms open wide, ready to welcome us back with a warm embrace.

⊙ My Thoughts

What worthless things distract or deter me from a deeper love for Christ? What can I do to return God to his rightful place on the throne of my heart? _____

_____

_____

_____

_____

♡ My Prayer

Loving heavenly Father, I praise you for your patience and kindness. I praise you because you have removed my sin from me as far as the east is from the west. Thank you for never giving up on me. Thank you for lovingly bringing me back to you. Show me the worthless idols I tend to put before you in my heart. Reveal to me those things that distract me and keep me from putting you first. Light a fire of passion in me so that I can love you with my whole heart. In Jesus' name I pray, amen.

This week I am praying for: _____

_____

_____

_____

_____

 My Choices

* This week I will choose to recognize God's loving voice calling me to himself.

* This week I will choose to turn from any worthless idols that captivate my heart.

* This week I will choose to love God with all my heart, mind, soul, and strength.

* This week I will choose to: _____

_____

_____

_____

_____

Couple's Discussion Starter

What things have we allowed to become idols in our lives?

For Further Reading: 2 KINGS 17–19

We easily fall into idolatry, for we are inclined
to it by nature; and coming to us by inheritance,
it seems pleasant.

—MARTIN LUTHER

41

Week 11

A High Calling of Great Trust

📖 Key Scripture: 1 Chronicles 9:23–27

These gatekeepers and their descendants, by their divisions, were responsible for guarding the entrance to the house of the LORD, the house that was formerly a tent. The gatekeepers were stationed on all four sides—east, west, north, and south. From time to time, their relatives in the villages came to share their duties for seven-day periods.

The four chief gatekeepers, all Levites, were in an office of great trust, for they were responsible for the rooms and treasuries at the house of God. They would spend the night around the house of God, since it was their duty to guard it. It was also their job to open the gates every morning.

 Reflection

Gatekeepers? If you're like me, you haven't spent a lot of time pondering the responsibilities of the gatekeepers for the Lord's house. That's unfortunate, because we can learn a unique lesson from the gatekeepers. Although their job may have seemed mundane compared to that of the high priest, these trusted officials had an important role in serving the Lord and their community. They were in charge of the rooms and treasuries of the house of the Lord. Not only did they maintain the temple and perform the day-to-day chores that kept it running, but they also guarded its treasures.

As I think about these persons of great trust, my mind races to the description of a noble wife in Proverbs 31. Solomon says, "Who can find a virtuous and capable wife? She is worth more than precious rubies. Her husband can trust her, and she will greatly enrich his life" (Proverbs 31:10–11).

Dear friend, do you see your role as a wife as a position of great trust and an opportunity to enrich your husband's life? Like the job of the gatekeeper, the responsibilities of being a wife may not seem glorious all the time. As positive wives, however, we need to see the bigger picture. Our worth is more than precious rubies, and our responsibility as trustworthy helpmates to our husbands is a high calling. May we desire to live up to it!

⊚ My Thoughts

In what areas can my husband completely trust me? Are there areas I need to work on in order to become more trustworthy? _____

_____

_____

_____

_____

♡ My Prayer

Holy God, I praise you, because you are a God of order, power, and strength. Thank you for the important responsibilities you gave to those who served in your Temple, from the high priest to the gatekeepers. Thank you for the high honor and great responsibility you have given to me as a wife. Help me to be trustworthy, and show me how to enrich my husband's life. Give me wisdom and strength to glorify you in my marriage. In Jesus' name I pray, amen.

This week I am praying for: _____

_____

_____

_____

_____

_____

_____

☀ My Choices

* This week I will choose to recognize the high calling of being a wife.

* This week I will choose to enrich my husband's life.

* This week I will choose to seek God's strength to be a person of great trust all the days of my life.

* This week I will choose to: _____

_____

_____

_____

_____

◗ Couple's Discussion Starter

Are we able to depend upon and trust each other in every area of our relationship? How do we enrich each other's lives?

📖 For Further Reading: 1 CHRONICLES 9–11

Responsibility is my response to God's ability.

—ALBERT J. LOWN

Week 12

The Beauty of Praise and Thanksgiving

📖 **Key Scripture:** Ezra 3:10–11

When the builders completed the foundation of the LORD's Temple, the priests put on their robes and took their places to blow their trumpets. And the Levites, descendants of Asaph, clashed their cymbals to praise the LORD, just as King David had prescribed. With praise and thanks, they sang this song to the LORD:

> *"He is so good!*
> *His faithful love for Israel endures forever!"*

Then all the people gave a great shout, praising the LORD because the foundation of the LORD's Temple had been laid.

The thankfulness of the receiver ought
to answer to the benefit of the bestower
as the echo answers to the voice.

—Thomas Fuller

 ## Reflection

It was a dream come true! Finally the Temple of the Lord was being rebuilt in Jerusalem. Once the foundation was complete, the Israelites paused for a time of thanksgiving and rejoicing. They still had a great deal of work ahead of them, but they recognized that giving thanks was an important part of the process.

I'm embarrassed to admit how many times I've forgotten to give thanks to God after a big accomplishment or major project in my life, not to mention all the little achievements along the way. And yet, here were the Israelites, stopping to give praise and thanksgiving right in the middle of their project! I want to be just as deliberate about giving glory to God, don't you? It doesn't take a lot of time to whisper a few sincere "thank yous" to God throughout the day.

When we continually give praise to God, we keep our eyes focused on what God has done instead of fretting over the possible difficulties ahead. When our hearts are filled with thanksgiving, it is easier for us to trust the Lord's guidance for the rest of our journey. Oh, the joy that floods the hearts of those who live with thanksgiving and praise continually on their lips! Let's determine to praise God—and not just when our journey is complete. Let's praise him right in the middle of it!

ⓞ My Thoughts

What qualities about my husband can I thank God for, knowing that God is not finished with him yet? _____

_____

_____

_____

_____

♡ My Prayer

Blessed Father, I praise you, for you alone are worthy of praise. There is none like you. You are my strength and my shield. You are my rock and my refuge. You are my help in time of need. You know all things and can do all things. I'm so thankful that you are with me and will never leave me. Thank you for the work that you are doing in my life. Thank you for my marriage and my husband. I praise you for the faithful, loving way that you have cared for me to this point in my life. I trust you for the rest of the journey. In Jesus' name, amen.

This week I am praying for:_____

_____

_____

_____

_____

_____

_____

☼ My Choices

* This week I will choose to praise and thank God continually throughout each day.

* This week I will choose to thank God for the wonderful qualities I see in my husband.

* This week I will choose to thank God for his provision in my life so far.

* This week I will choose to: _____

_____

_____

_____

_____

⟨ Couple's Discussion Starter

What can we stop and thank God for right now in our lives, even if the situation is not yet resolved, or the job is not yet complete?

📖 For Further Reading: PSALMS 103–106

In thanking God, we fasten upon his favors to us;
in praising and adoring God, we fasten upon
his perfections in himself.

—MATTHEW HENRY

Week 13

Humble Prayer

📖 **Key Scripture:** NEHEMIAH 1:5–9

Then I said, "O LORD, God of heaven, the great and awesome God who keeps his covenant of unfailing love with those who love him and obey his commands, listen to my prayer! Look down and see me praying night and day for your people Israel. I confess that we have sinned against you. Yes, even my own family and I have sinned! We have sinned terribly by not obeying the commands, laws, and regulations that you gave us through your servant Moses.

"Please remember what you told your servant Moses: 'If you sin, I will scatter you among the nations. But if you return to me and obey my commands, even if you are exiled to the ends of the earth, I will bring you back to the place I have chosen for my name to be honored.'"

Prayer is not conquering God's reluctance,
but taking hold upon God's willingness.

—PHILLIPS BROOKS

 Reflection

Nehemiah offers a tremendous example of an effective prayer from a man who clearly felt unworthy yet boldly and sincerely approached the Lord. Notice that Nehemiah began with praise to God, "who keeps his covenant of unfailing love." What a glorious way to approach our heavenly Father! Next, Nehemiah humbly confessed that not only had the nation of Israel sinned, but he and his family had also sinned against God. He asked for God's mercy, standing confidently on God's Word with his request. He reminded God (as if God needed reminding) of what he had promised: that if the Israelites returned to him and obeyed his commands, then he would bring them back to his chosen land.

God answered Nehemiah's prayer in a miraculous way by moving in the heart of King Artaxerxes and clearing the way for Nehemiah to return to Jerusalem to rebuild the Temple. My friend, don't be afraid to approach God's throne of grace with your humble prayer. Follow Nehemiah's example. Start with praise and thanksgiving, move on to confession, and then make your requests based upon God's Word. God loves to hear the prayers of his people!

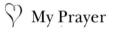 My Thoughts

Is there anything I need to confess before God? What needs have I been withholding from God in prayer?

_____

_____

_____

_____

_____

♡ My Prayer

Sovereign God, magnificent Lord, I praise you for your unfailing love and mercy toward those who obey you. Thank you for welcoming your people with open arms. I confess that I have sinned against you and disobeyed you. Help me to turn from my sin and obey your commands. Please work in a powerful way in my life. Thank you for hearing my prayer. I trust that in your loving-kindness, you will answer in the way you know is best. In Jesus' name, amen.

This week I am praying for: _____

_____

_____

_____

_____

_____

_____

☼ My Choices

* This week I will choose to confess my sin and turn from it.

* This week I will choose to sincerely and specifically bring my requests before God.

* This week I will choose to be diligent to pray daily for my needs and the needs of others.

* This week I will choose to: _____

_____

_____

_____

_____

◗ Couple's Discussion Starter

Is there any request or confession we need to lay before the Lord together as a couple?

📖 For Further Reading: NEHEMIAH 1–3

Man is never so tall as when he kneels before
God—never so great as when he humbles himself
before God. And the man who kneels to God
can stand up to anything.

—LOUIS H. EVANS

Week 14

Glorious Security

📖 Key Scripture: ESTHER 2:16–18

When Esther was taken to King Xerxes at the royal palace in early winter of the seventh year of his reign, the king loved her more than any of the other young women. He was so delighted with her that he set the royal crown on her head and declared her queen instead of Vashti. To celebrate the occasion, he gave a banquet in Esther's honor for all his princes and servants, giving generous gifts to everyone and declaring a public festival for the provinces.

Faith means trusting in advance
what will only make sense in reverse.

—PHILIP YANCEY

 Reflection

In our passage today, we find Esther in what appears to be a glorious place. Xerxes, the king of Media and Persia, certainly loved and adored her. He even declared a holiday in her honor. If only we could live out all the days of our marriages in similar wedding-day bliss! It seemed that Esther would be happy forever in her position as queen.

Then her circumstances changed. The Israelites, who were living in exile in Persia, were being threatened with death. An Israelite herself, Esther was the only person in a position to appeal to the king. The problem was, she had not been invited to see the king in over a month—imagine that, after Xerxes made such a great declaration of love!—and anyone who approached the king without an invitation put his or her life on the line.

What did Esther do? She took her insecurity to the only one who could provide security: God. She asked the Israelites to pray and fast for three days. She recognized that her life was in God's hands.

What do you do with your insecurities? Do you take them to your loving heavenly Father, or do you try to handle your circumstances yourself? Perhaps your marriage, like Esther's, has moved away from wedding-day spectacular and settled into a distant connection. There is hope! God worked in a miraculous way in Esther's life when she cried out for help and then left the results to him. Let's be positive, courageous wives who place our hope and security in God. People and circumstances may not be secure, but our God is faithful and unchanging.

ⓖ My Thoughts

Do I find my security in my husband or in the Lord? How often do I try to handle my fears and insecurities myself when I should be taking them to God? _____

_____

_____

_____

♡ My Prayer

Mighty Lord, I praise you, because you are my rock and my refuge. I can run to you and find strength and hope. Thank you for always being with me and for the great security I feel in you. I trust your love for me. Father, I ask that you continue to strengthen and renew my marriage. Help me to keep my eyes on you, for you are trustworthy and unchanging. I love you, Lord. In Jesus' name I pray, amen.

This week I am praying for: _____

_____

_____

_____

_____

_____

☼ My Choices

* This week I will choose to recognize areas of insecurity in my life and take them to the Lord.

* This week I will choose to trust God with my life and rest in his mighty hands.

* This week I will choose to bring renewed hope into my marriage relationship.

* This week I will choose to: _____

_____

_____

_____

_____

◊ Couple's Discussion Starter

Are there any areas in our relationship where we have grown distant and need to come back together in renewed love and commitment?

📖 For Further Reading: ESTHER 4–6

This only can my fears control,
and bid my sorrows fly;
What harm can ever reach my soul
beneath my Father's eye?

—ANNE STEELE

Week 15

God Almighty

📖 Key Scripture: Job 38:28–33

Does the rain have a father? Where does dew come from? Who is the mother of the ice? Who gives birth to the frost from the heavens? For the water turns to ice as hard as rock, and the surface of the water freezes.

Can you hold back the movements of the stars? Are you able to restrain the Pleiades or Orion? Can you ensure the proper sequence of the seasons or guide the constellation of the Bear with her cubs across the heavens? Do you know the laws of the universe and how God rules the earth?

We cannot know all about God
for the obvious reason that the finite
cannot comprehend the infinite.

—R. B. KUIPER

 ## Reflection

Aren't you glad that God is in charge of the world and we aren't? God gave Job a gentle reminder that God is the creator of the universe; he knows all things and can do all things. Honestly, we all may need that little reminder now and then. As women, we tend to take the weight of the world on our shoulders. We often believe, "My way is the best way," or, "If I don't do it, no one else will." We can be guilty of pushing God to the side in order to take charge ourselves.

This is especially true when it comes to our husbands. We want to change them, fix them, and teach them—our way, right now! Yet God has work to do in their lives (and in ours), and it may be a slow process. As positive wives, we need to trust that God knows what he is doing, and he knows what is best.

After all, if God can run the universe, he can handle the difficulties and struggles in our lives and our marriages. When Job went through a series of painful tragedies, the bigger picture wasn't evident to him. And so it can be with us; we may not understand why God is allowing us to go through certain trials. We can't fix everything, but we *can* fall into the hands of the God who sees all and knows all and rest in the knowledge that we are his. Certainly, he gives us responsibilities and work to do—but we must leave the final results to him.

⊚ My Thoughts

Am I trying to play God in a situation or in a person's life right now? What about in my husband's life? _____

_____

_____

_____

_____

♡ My Prayer

Powerful God, creator of the universe, I praise you. You are a sovereign God. You know all things and can do all things. Thank you for caring about the details of my life. Thank you for holding me so lovingly in your hands. I confess that I sometimes try to take control in areas of my life that need to be given over to you. Take the people and the situations in my life and use them for your glory. I give them to you, recognizing that I don't know what you know, and I can't do what you do. I praise you, for you alone are worthy of praise. In Jesus' name, amen.

This week I am praying for: _____

_____

_____

_____

_____

_____

_____

☼ My Choices

* This week I will choose to recognize areas where I try to take charge and fix things beyond my control.

* This week I will choose to give those areas over to God and rest in his care.

* This week I will choose to do the work God has given me and leave the final results to him.

* This week I will choose to: _____

_____

_____

_____

_____

◊ Couple's Discussion Starter

In what areas do we allow God to control our marriage? Are there any areas where we are pushing God aside and trying to take control ourselves?

📖 For Further Reading: Job 38–42

God's decrees, impossible to be resisted,
and leaving us in the dark as to what may come next,
are calculated to fill the mind with holy awe.

—ALBERT BARNES

Week 16

They Cried and He Satisfied

📖 Key Scripture: PSALM 107:4–9

Some wandered in the desert,
lost and homeless.
Hungry and thirsty,
they nearly died.
"LORD, help!" they cried in their trouble,
and he rescued them from their distress.
He led them straight to safety,
to a city where they could live.
Let them praise the LORD for his great love
and for all his wonderful deeds to them.
For he satisfies the thirsty
and fills the hungry with good things.

No heart of a child of God will ever be
satisfied with any object or person short
of the Lord Jesus Christ.

—CHARLES H. SPURGEON

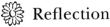 ## Reflection

Hungry, thirsty, and desperate. Perhaps you have never been in a terribly low situation like the one described in today's passage, but I'm sure you have been through times of despair in your life. Maybe you lost a loved one, or someone abandoned you, or you went through a financial disaster. Maybe you simply felt overwhelmed with too many responsibilities circling around you.

When times like these come, we need to remember: no matter what challenges we face, they are never too big or overwhelming for God. The Israelites cried out to God in the depths of despair, and he rescued them. He led them to a new place where they could live in safety. We may not understand why we experience a difficult situation, but we do know we can cry out to God for help. He desires for us to turn to him, and he is ready and willing to help.

I love the last verse in our passage: "He satisfies the thirsty and fills the hungry with good things." Are you thirsty? Come to the river that never runs dry. Is there a hunger inside of you? Come feast at the Lord's table of abundance, for he satisfies our needs. May we say with the psalmist, "Praise the LORD for his great love, for he has done wonderful things!"

⑥ My Thoughts

What do I do when I am desperate or in need? Do I cry out to God, seeking him for satisfaction? Or do I run to someone or something else, hoping that person or thing will satisfy my need? _____

_____

_____

_____

_____

_____

♡ My Prayer

Wonderful heavenly Father, thank you for your loving care for me. Thank you that your love satisfies. I'm so grateful that I can come to you when things are good and cry out to you in times of need. I praise you because you alone are able to bring me out of despair and into a place of safety and rest. My eyes are on you for help and hope. In Jesus' name I pray, amen.

This week I am praying for: _____

_____

_____

_____

_____

_____

_____

☼ My Choices

* This week I will choose to cry out to God with my needs, whether great or small.

* This week I will choose to look to God to satisfy the longings in my heart.

* This week I will choose to praise the Lord for his great love and care for me.

* This week I will choose to: _____

_____

_____

_____

_____

◗ Couple's Discussion Starter

Have we had times in our life together when we felt desperate and didn't know where to turn? What did we do?

📖 For Further Reading: PSALMS 46–49

God's chief gift to those
who seek Him is Himself.

—E. B. PUSEY

Week 17

Overflow of the Heart

📖 **Key Scripture:** PROVERBS 4:23–27

Above all else, guard your heart, for it affects everything you do.

Avoid all perverse talk; stay far from corrupt speech.

Look straight ahead, and fix your eyes on what lies before you. Mark out a straight path for your feet; then stick to the path and stay safe. Don't get sidetracked; keep your feet from following evil.

The keeping and right managing
of the heart in every condition, is one great
business of a Christian's life.

—JOHN FLAVEL

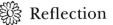 ## Reflection

Why does Solomon tell us to guard our hearts? Because the passions and desires of the heart often dictate our direction and what we choose to do. If our desires are righteous and glorifying to God, they lead us down a path of wisdom and delight. But if we get distracted and begin to fix our hearts' desires on evil, we are led down a path of destruction. What are the distractions in your life? What tempts you to get off the path God has prepared for you or directs your feet away from his best for you? Solomon tells us to look straight ahead and fix our eyes on what lies before us. Don't get distracted or sidetracked, Solomon says. Stay on a safe path!

Solomon also encourages us to watch our mouths and stay away from corrupt speech. It's so easy to start down a path of destruction with our mouths—telling a half-truth, sharing gossip, grumbling about our husbands, and the list goes on. Our words are an overflow of what is in our hearts. When we guard our hearts, our speech is pleasant. May the Lord create clean hearts in us, so that we may speak wisely and walk down a straight path with him!

⊚ My Thoughts

What are the desires of my heart? Am I following certain passions or pursuits that will lead me down a path of destruction? _____

_____

_____

_____

_____

♡ My Prayer

Holy and wonderful Father, I praise you for your righteousness and wisdom. Your ways are perfect, and your paths are straight. Alert me to desires in my heart that are not pleasing to you. Give me the strength to turn from them. Create in me a clean heart, O God, and renew a right spirit within me, so that I may walk in paths of righteousness and glorify you with my life. Put a guard over my tongue, so that I may honor you with my words. I love you, Lord. In Jesus' name, amen.

This week I am praying for: _____

_____

_____

_____

_____

_____

☼ My Choices

* This week I will choose to guard my heart and recognize desires that are not pleasing to God.

* This week I will choose to honor God with my words and not hurt others with them.

* This week I will choose to keep my eyes on the path before me and not get sidetracked by evil.

* This week I will choose to: _____

_____

_____

_____

_____

✎ Couple's Discussion Starter

What are some specific ways we can each guard our hearts against evil?

📖 For Further Reading: PROVERBS 1–4

The heart is the warehouse, the hand and tongue are
but the shops; what is in these comes from thence—
the heart contrives and the members execute.

—ARTHUR W. PINK

Week 18

No Know-It-Alls

📖 **Key Scripture:** ECCLESIASTES 8:16–17

In my search for wisdom, I tried to observe everything that goes on all across the earth. I discovered that there is ceaseless activity, day and night. This reminded me that no one can discover everything God has created in our world, no matter how hard they work at it. Not even the wisest people know everything, even if they say they do.

If all the works of God were such that human reason could easily grasp them, they would not be called wonderful or beyond the power of words to tell.

—THOMAS À KEMPIS

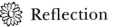 Reflection

Even the wisest man in the world can't claim to know it all. No one can fathom everything about God and his ways. God's thoughts are higher than our thoughts, and his ways are different from ours. And yet, don't we all try to figure out God at times? We think we know what he is up to, and we're disappointed when he doesn't work things out the way we think he should. When a tragedy happens, someone is neglected, or a person is hurt, we often wonder, *Where is God?* We are tempted to think that God just doesn't care, or he dropped the ball, or he's angry with us.

As positive wives, we must humbly realize that we can't figure out the ways of God. Certainly we can learn more about his character by reading what he has revealed about himself in his Word; but we can't begin to comprehend everything he is doing or why he allows certain things to play out the way they do. So let's stop trying! Instead, let's place our trust in what we do know about him: he is a God of love, justice, power, and righteousness.

Don't make the mistake of putting God in a little box of your own understanding. Remember that he is the Sovereign Lord who knows all things and can do all things. We may think we know what is best, but ultimately the Lord of all the universe knows best. Let's rest in the fact that our lives are in good hands.

⊚ My Thoughts

When have I been disappointed with God because I couldn't figure out why he allowed something to happen?

_____

_____

_____

_____

_____

♡ My Prayer

Sovereign and powerful God, I praise you, because you know all things and can do all things. I praise you for your love and care for me. Your ways are perfect! Thank you that even though I can't know all your plans or understand all your ways, I can trust your love, power, righteousness, and justice. Thank you for having a plan and a purpose for me. I confess that I often think I know what is best; but you, Lord, are the one who knows. I trust you with my life. In Jesus' name, amen.

This week I am praying for: _____

_____

_____

_____

_____

_____

_____

☼ My Choices

* This week I will choose to recognize that I cannot figure out God.

* This week I will choose to thank God for his perfect ways.

* This week I will choose to trust God's care even when I don't understand his ways.

* This week I will choose to: _____

_____

_____

_____

_____

◗ Couple's Discussion Starter

Why are people always trying to figure out God? Do we trust God even when we don't understand what he is doing?

📖 For Further Reading: ISAIAH 54–55

Because God knows all things perfectly,
He knows no thing better than any other thing,
but all things equally well. He never discovers anything,
He is never surprised, never amazed.

—A. W. TOZER

Week 19

A King's Affection

📖 Key Scripture: SONG OF SONGS 1:1–4

This is Solomon's song of songs, more wonderful than any other.

Young Woman: "Kiss me again and again, for your love is sweeter than wine. How fragrant your cologne, and how pleasing your name! No wonder all the young women love you! Take me with you. Come, let's run! Bring me into your bedroom, O my king."

This is one of the miracles of love; it gives—
to both, but perhaps especially to the woman—
a power of seeing through its own enchantments
and yet not being disenchanted.

—C. S. LEWIS

 Reflection

Isn't that the way you talk with *your* husband? If you're like most wives, you may have sounded like the young woman in Song of Songs on your wedding night, but somehow you've moved on to other loving words—like "Take out the trash," or "Why haven't you fixed the disposal yet?" Take a moment to think how your husband would respond if you spoke the kind of loving words we find in today's passage. After he got over the initial shock, he probably would warm up to them quite nicely!

The truth is, when we make our husbands feel like attractive kings, they are going to be attracted to us as queens. So let's renew those early fires. Let's determine to talk with our husbands in a loving manner and spend more time lifting them up than nagging and complaining. Sure, if we've been married for more than a few weeks, we have discovered some of our spouses' faults. But we can choose to overlook those faults—just as we hope they are overlooking ours.

Our husbands need to hear that we desire them. They want to know we think they're wonderful. They need to feel that we respect them and adore them. We all desire our husbands' love, right? Let's follow the example of the wife in Song of Songs and tell them how much their love means to us.

⟳ My Thoughts

How do I make my husband feel like a king? In what ways do I let him know I enjoy his affection? _____

_____

_____

_____

_____

_____

♡ My Prayer

Loving heavenly Father, I praise you, for you are a God of love. You show us how to love each other. Thank you for giving me my husband. Help me to appreciate his good qualities, and give me a blind eye to some of his weaknesses. Develop a deeper, more passionate relationship between us. Show me how to bring out the best in him. Most important, let your grace-filled love pour through me to him. In Jesus' name I pray, amen.

This week I am praying for: _____

_____

_____

_____

_____

_____

_____

☼ My Choices

* This week I will choose to talk lovingly and admiringly to my husband.

* This week I will choose to focus on my husband's positive qualities and overlook his negatives.

* This week I will choose to let my husband know how much I enjoy his affection and love toward me.

* This week I will choose to: _____

_____

_____

_____

_____

◖ Couple's Discussion Starter

What first attracted us to each other?

📖 For Further Reading: SONG OF SONGS 7–8

That is the true season of love, when we believe that we alone can love, that no one could ever have loved so before us, and that no one will love in the same way after us.

—JOHANN WOLFGANG VON GOETHE

Week 20

Perfect Peace

📖 Key Scripture: Isaiah 26:3–4, 8–9

You will keep in perfect peace all who trust in you,
whose thoughts are fixed on you!
Trust in the LORD always,
for the LORD GOD is the eternal Rock. . . .
LORD, we love to obey your laws;
our heart's desire is to glorify your name.
All night long I search for you;
earnestly I seek for God.
For only when you come to judge the earth
will people turn from wickedness and do what is right.

All men desire peace,
but all do not care for the things
that go to make true peace.

—THOMAS À KEMPIS

 Reflection

When was the last time you were stressed? If you're like most women, you don't have to think very far back! Every day seems to come with its own portion of stressors. The problem isn't so much the stress itself; it's what we do when we have too much stress. Do we go over and over all the details of the circumstances in our minds? Do we worry and fret? Do we complain?

The words we just read from Isaiah 26 lead us to a place of peace—to our eternal Rock. God gives us perfect peace when we fix our thoughts on him. When we turn our eyes upward to the God of peace, we begin to see our circumstances in a different light. Suddenly what seemed so important isn't worth the anxiety anymore, because we're looking at it from the eternal perspective of what really matters to God.

As we keep our eyes on God, cast our cares on him, and bring all our concerns to him in prayer, we experience a calm that passes all understanding. Notice the words in our passage today: "All night long I search for you; earnestly I seek for God." Fixing our thoughts on God is a continual practice, not a quick, one-time prayer. As we continually seek him, God meets us where we are and lovingly holds our hands through our challenges and difficulties. Let's turn our eyes toward him and seek his wisdom, direction, and peace.

⊚ My Thoughts

When I am stressed, do I fix my thoughts on God, or do I fret and worry? How can I begin to handle my stress in a more positive way? _____

_____

_____

_____

_____

♡ My Prayer

God of peace, I praise you for the peace you bring to my life. I am weak, but you are strong. I tend to worry, but you bring great calm to my spirit. Thank you for loving me, protecting me, and providing for me. Help me to continually fix my thoughts on you, High King of heaven. I long for you. I earnestly seek you. Help me to keep my eyes fixed upon you and to see my circumstances from your eternal perspective. In Jesus' name I pray, amen.

This week I am praying for: _____

_____

_____

_____

_____

_____

_____

_____

☼ My Choices

* This week I will choose to earnestly seek God by fixing my thoughts on him.

* This week I will choose to ask for God's peace in the areas where I tend to fret.

* This week I will choose to show my trust in God by obeying his laws.

* This week I will choose to: _____
  _____
  _____
  _____
  _____

◊ Couple's Discussion Starter

In what areas of our lives do we need to experience peace right now?

📖 For Further Reading: ISAIAH 40

The peace of God will keep us from sinning under our troubles and from sinking under them.

—MATTHEW HENRY

Week 21

Bragging Rights

📖 Key Scripture: JEREMIAH 9:23–24

This is what the LORD says: "Let not the wise man gloat in his wisdom, or the mighty man in his might, or the rich man in his riches. Let them boast in this alone: that they truly know me and understand that I am the LORD who is just and righteous, whose love is unfailing, and that I delight in these things. I, the LORD, have spoken!"

The Christian is strong or weak
depending upon how closely he has
cultivated the knowledge of God.

—A. W. TOZER

 Reflection

What are you proud of? No, really, what makes you gloat? Take a moment to honestly identify an area of your life that causes you to feel pride in your heart. It's a little different for each of us. Some women are proud of their outward appearance or their children's accomplishments or their husbands' jobs or their big houses. Others brag about their long list of activities or the number of committees they chair.

But Jeremiah's message from God is plain and to the point: there is only one thing worth pursuing—only one thing worth boasting about. God wants us to know him and understand that he is the Lord. He delights when we recognize his unfailing love and acknowledge the justice and righteousness he brings to the earth.

For most of us, "knowing and understanding God" isn't at the top of our boasting lists. We tend to get caught up in things that make us look good or smart or powerful and forget what's really important: a thriving relationship with God. Our glory shouldn't be in the riches we accumulate or the power we avail or the wisdom we achieve. What matters in life is knowing God, because he is eternal. All earthly fame and fortune will pass away, but our relationship with God will last forever. As positive wives, let's make God our supreme pursuit. Everything else will fall into its proper place of importance.

⊚ My Thoughts

What are some of the outward things I tend to take pride in? Am I willing to pursue God first and set aside the need to brag about these other things? _____

_____

_____

_____

_____

♡ My Prayer

Holy, loving, and perfect Father, I praise you for your unfailing love. I praise you for your righteousness and justice. I praise you for being a glorious and knowable God. Thank you for caring about my relationship with you. I confess that I have been proud of _____ _____. My desire is to draw closer to you and walk in a deeper relationship with you. Help me to pursue you with my whole heart. I want to boast in you alone! In Jesus' name, amen.

This week I am praying for: _____

_____

_____

_____

_____

_____

☼ My Choices

* This week I will choose to recognize areas of pride in my life.

* This week I will choose to pursue a deeper relationship with Christ.

* This week I will choose to find my delight in the Lord and not in other things.

* This week I will choose to: _____

_____

_____

_____

_____

✒ Couple's Discussion Starter

What things in our lives are we most proud of right now? Have we ever thought of boasting about knowing and understanding God?

📖 For Further Reading: JEREMIAH 9–10

The nearer we come to God,
the more graciously will he reveal himself to us.

—CHARLES H. SPURGEON

Week 22

No Pit-Free Guarantee

📖 **Key Scripture:** LAMENTATIONS 3:49–57

My tears flow down endlessly. They will not stop until the LORD looks down from heaven and sees. My heart is breaking over the fate of all the women of Jerusalem.

My enemies, whom I have never harmed, chased me like a bird. They threw me into a pit and dropped stones on me. The water flowed above my head, and I cried out, "This is the end!"

But I called on your name, LORD, from deep within the well, and you heard me! You listened to my pleading; you heard my weeping! Yes, you came at my despairing cry and told me, "Do not fear."

The more we are afflicted by adversities,
the surer we are made of our fellowship with Christ.

—JOHN CALVIN

🌼 Reflection

Does God intend for all of his people to be happy, prosperous, and successful? In our passage today, we see that even a prophet of God is not exempt from the pits of life. Jeremiah was down—way down—in the dumps. Life wasn't happy or prosperous for him. The fact is, most of God's servants throughout the Bible and throughout history experienced tragedy, pain, and loss.

Now, I don't want to sound as if I only have negative expectations of life, but I do want to have realistic ones. As followers of Christ, we have no guarantee that we will experience easy, wonderful, or successful lives. The beauty of Jeremiah's lamentation is that he cried out to God, and God heard him and delivered him from the pit. Perhaps your life hasn't turned out the way you wanted it to. Maybe your marriage is difficult, and you feel entitled to have a better husband or a happier life. Cry out to God! God doesn't guarantee us a pit-free life, but he does tell us he is with us. He will hear our prayers and help us through the storm.

Can the pits of life be positive? They may not feel positive when we're in the midst of them, but we can have hope that something good will come from even the worst of circumstances. Our God is a redeeming God. He not only rescues us from the depths of despair, but he brings good out of bad situations. Let's ask the God of hope to

free us from our fears and transform us into truly positive
wives.

(◎) My Thoughts

Am I disillusioned or angry with God for allowing a par-
ticular difficulty or challenge in my life? _____

_____

_____

_____

_____

(♡) My Prayer

Sovereign God, mighty Lord, I praise you, for you have all
wisdom and power. I praise you for you are the High King
of heaven, and you know what you're doing. Thank you
for your many blessings in my life. Thank you for never
leaving me. Thank you for hearing my cry and rescuing
my life from the pit. Thank you for your tender care during the difficult times. Thank you that I can call to you for
help and strength each day. In Jesus' name I pray, amen.

This week I am praying for: _____

_____

_____

_____

_____

_____

☼ My Choices

* This week I will choose to thank God for his constant presence in my life.

* This week I will choose to recognize that life isn't always going to be easy or go my way.

* This week I will choose to ask God to free me from my fear and bring hope into my heart.

* This week I will choose to: _____

_____

_____

_____

_____

🖋 Couple's Discussion Starter

Why do most people feel entitled to an easy and trouble-free life? What expectations do we have?

📖 For Further Reading: LAMENTATIONS 1–3

Afflictions are sent for this end, to bring us to
the throne of grace, to teach us to pray and to
make the word of God's grace precious to us.

—MATTHEW HENRY

Week 23

It's Alive!

📖 Key Scripture: EZEKIEL 37:1–6

The LORD took hold of me, and I was carried away by the Spirit of the LORD to a valley filled with bones. He led me around among the old, dry bones that covered the valley floor. They were scattered everywhere across the ground. Then he asked me, "Son of man, can these bones become living people again?"

"O Sovereign LORD," I replied, "you alone know the answer to that."

Then he said to me, "Speak to these bones and say, 'Dry bones, listen to the word of the LORD! This is what the Sovereign LORD says: Look! I am going to breathe into you and make you live again! I will put flesh and muscles on you and cover you with skin. I will put breath into you, and you will come to life. Then you will know that I am the LORD.'"

> What oxygen is to the lungs,
> such is hope to the meaning of life.
>
> —EMIL BRUNNER

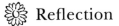 Reflection

Ezekiel 37 has the makings of a modern-day horror movie—dry, dead bones that come alive again with muscles and ligaments and flesh! What was God telling the Israelites through this illustration? He was reminding them that although they were scattered and divided as a nation, he would breathe new life into them. The sovereign God of all creation is able to bring life into anything! Is your marriage dead? God can bring it back to life. Are your feelings dead? God can restore your passion. Is there a situation in your life where you have lost hope? God is able to breathe fresh air into what is dead and create a rejuvenated spirit within you.

When we lose hope, we are tempted to give up. As positive wives, however, we must never lose sight of the fact that God is able. The very same God who resurrected his Son from the dead is able to revive us and our circumstances. He makes all things new, for he is a redeeming God! Of course, there are some dead things that God chooses not to bring back to life; but even in those times, he injects a redeeming factor. Just as a beautiful flower emerges from a seed that falls to the ground and dies, so God brings forth something beautiful and good from our lifeless situations. Persist in faithful prayer, and watch what the God of all wonders is able to do!

 My Thoughts

Is there an area in my life right now that seems dead? Am I willing to seek God's restoration and renewal in the situation? _____

_____

_____

_____

_____

♡ My Prayer

Redeeming God, I praise you, for you breathe new life into the dead. You restore hopeless situations and resurrect dead passions. Revive my heart! Make me new. Bring me to a place of renewed passion for you and for others. Help me to recognize what is worthwhile and what is unnecessary. Keep me from trying to resurrect those things that are meaningless for your kingdom's sake. I trust you and thank you for the hope that you bring. In Jesus' name, amen.

This week I am praying for: _____

_____

_____

_____

_____

_____

_____

☼ My Choices

* This week I will choose to find my hope in the sovereign God who is able to renew all things.

* This week I will choose to give over the dead areas of my life to him.

* This week I will choose to rejoice in what is meaningful and worthy.

* This week I will choose to: _____

_____

_____

_____

_____

✒ Couple's Discussion Starter

What are some practical ways that we can encourage each other to have hope in God when circumstances in life seem hopeless?

📖 For Further Reading: EZEKIEL 36–37

*What an excellent ground of hope and confidence,
when we reflect upon these three things in prayer, the
Father's love, the Son's merit, and the Spirit's power!*

—THOMAS MANTON

Week 24

The Beloved's Prayer

📖 Key Scripture: DANIEL 9:20–23

I went on praying and confessing my sin and the sins of my people, pleading with the LORD my God for Jerusalem, his holy mountain. As I was praying, Gabriel, whom I had seen in the earlier vision, came swiftly to me at the time of the evening sacrifice. He explained to me, "Daniel, I have come here to give you insight and understanding. The moment you began praying, a command was given. I am here to tell you what it was, for God loves you very much. Now listen, so you can understand the meaning of your vision."

The fellowship of God
is delightful beyond all telling.

—A. W. TOZER

🌼 Reflection

What a beautiful prayer—and an amazing answer to prayer! Can you imagine humbly praying to God and an angel comes to talk with you and reassure you? Gabriel told Daniel that he was greatly loved by God. As followers of Christ, you and I are greatly loved by God too. We are his beloved. It's tempting to think that God only hears the prayers of "perfect people" like Daniel and not sinners like us. But notice that Daniel was a fellow sinner. He began his prayer with confession of his sin.

My fellow sinner, if you have placed your faith in Christ, you are forgiven through what Christ did on the cross. You are a child of God, one of his precious ones. Cast your cares on him. Don't allow false assumptions to hold you back. Like Daniel, you and I can humbly come before our loving heavenly Father, confess our sins, and bring our requests. We may not receive as dramatic a response as Daniel, but we can rest assured that the God who loves us also hears us. He is with us and has a plan for our lives.

When we face difficulties and challenges, we need to remember that Daniel faced challenges too. (Remember the lion's den?) The fact that we're in a difficult situation doesn't mean that God loves us less than someone else who has a seemingly trouble-free life. Let's steer clear of comparing ourselves to others when it comes to our spirituality or God's love. Instead, let's remember that we are precious to God and seek his power and grace for our unique life journeys.

◎ My Thoughts

Do I see myself as precious to God, or do I tend to assume that God loves others more than me, because their lives are going well? _____

_____

_____

_____

_____

♡ My Prayer

Holy and amazing God, I praise you for your love and mercy. Thank you for sending your son, Jesus. Thank you for his sacrifice on the cross that allows me to stand forgiven before you. Thank you for leading me to place my faith in Christ, and thank you for the transforming work you have done and are doing in my life. Thank you for allowing me to be one of your beloved, precious, and dearly loved children. I love you, Father. In Jesus' name I pray, amen.

This week I am praying for: _____

_____

_____

_____

_____

☼ My Choices

* This week I will choose to thank God for his precious love for me.

* This week I will choose to guard myself from comparing my spirituality to others'.

* This week I will choose to pray with confidence, knowing that God hears my prayers.

* This week I will choose to: _____

_____

_____

_____

_____

✒ Couple's Discussion Starter

As a couple, how can we be more committed to prayer like Daniel?

📖 For Further Reading: DANIEL 9–10

We are the Beloved. We are intimately loved long before our parents, teachers, spouses, children and friends loved or wounded us. That's the truth of our lives. That's the truth I want you to claim for yourself. That's the truth spoken by the voice that says, "You are my Beloved."

—HENRI NOUWEN

Week 25

A Father's Gentle Call

📖 Key Scripture: HOSEA 11:1–4

When Israel was a child, I loved him as a son, and I called my son out of Egypt. But the more I called to him, the more he rebelled, offering sacrifices to the images of Baal and burning incense to idols. It was I who taught Israel how to walk, leading him along by the hand. But he doesn't know or even care that it was I who took care of him. I led Israel along with my ropes of kindness and love. I lifted the yoke from his neck, and I myself stooped to feed him.

God's favorite word is—come!

—ROBERT L. STERNER

🌼 Reflection

Take a moment to envision the precious picture of God tenderly calling his people to himself. He offers the illustration of a gentle parent lovingly leading his child in the right direction. God doesn't scream his demands; he kindly calls his people to draw near. God said through his servant Hosea that he taught the Israelites how to walk, led them by the hand, and stooped to feed them. Isn't that beautiful?

Sadly, even though God graciously, lovingly cared for his own, they did not listen to him. It's hard to believe that someone would turn away and reject such a tender call, but the Israelites were enticed by the gods of the culture around them. Hmmm . . . could that be a description of us today? God still calls us in his gentle, quiet voice, but often we don't listen, because we're pulled by the temptations of this world. We may not worship Baal or other foreign gods, but we do get sidetracked from our devotion to God by people and things we think will satisfy the longings in our hearts.

As positive wives, let's commit to hearing God's loving voice and not turn away in our own direction. Just as kind parents reach out to give their children a hand and help them along life's way, so our heavenly Father desires to take us by the hand and lead us in the way we should go. His paths are best. May we go hand in hand with him!

 My Thoughts

Am I following God's leading in my life right now, or am I ignoring his voice? _____

_____

_____

_____

_____

♡ My Prayer

Gracious and loving heavenly Father, thank you for caring about your people. Thank you for caring about me. I praise you for your love, which goes far beyond an earthly parent's love. Your love is perfect. You are patient and kind. You guide me along the right path. Help me listen to your voice as you gently lead me. Alert me to times when I am going my own way, and bring me back to you. I love you and want to follow you. In Jesus' name I pray, amen.

This week I am praying for: _____

_____

_____

_____

_____

_____

_____

☼ My Choices

* This week I will choose to see God as my loving heavenly Father.

* This week I will choose to hear God's voice and follow his lead.

* This week I will choose to be aware of distractions that keep me from growing in my relationship with the Lord.

* This week I will choose to: _____

_____

_____

_____

_____

_____

◗ Couple's Discussion Starter

How have we felt God's gentle leading in our lives and in our relationship?

📖 For Further Reading: HOSEA 10–11

Our total welfare is the constant concern
of God's loving heart.

—W. J. C. WHITE

Week 26

Expressions of His Grace

📖 Key Scripture: JOEL 2:20–24

"I will remove these armies from the north and send them far away. I will drive them back into the parched waste-lands, where they will die. Those in the rear will go into the Dead Sea; those at the front will go into the Mediter-ranean. The stench of their rotting bodies will rise over the land."

Surely the LORD has done great things! Don't be afraid, my people! Be glad now and rejoice because the LORD has done great things. Don't be afraid, you animals of the field! The pastures will soon be green. The trees will again be filled with luscious fruit; fig trees and grapevines will flourish once more. Rejoice, you people of Jerusalem! Rejoice in the LORD your God! For the rains he sends are an expression of his grace. Once more the autumn rains will come, as well as the rains of spring. The threshing floors will again be piled high with grain, and the presses will overflow with wine and olive oil.

❀ Reflection

As sure as the changing of the seasons, so sure is God's grace for us! He brings wonder and beauty to every season of our lives. He provides, he protects, he creates. Let's hear the message of Joel, my dear sisters in Christ: "The LORD has done great things! Don't be afraid. . . . Be glad now and rejoice!"

Our passage today inspires a positive outlook on life and a joyful perspective in every situation. As we observe who God is and what he has done, we can choose to turn from fear and rejoice in him. The Bible is filled from Old Testament to New Testament with encouragement to rejoice in the Lord. Fear grows when our eyes are on our circumstances. Disappointment develops when our eyes are on people. But when our eyes are on the Lord, we can say with the psalmist, "Those who look to him . . . will be radiant with joy" (Psalm 34:5).

Let us live with an attitude of expectancy of what God will do. Let's bring joy to our families, our friends, and everyone around us, as we focus on God's hope and allow it to shine brightly through us. We have a choice to be fretful and angry or faith-filled and joyful. This one attitude choice can make a powerful difference in our lives as women and as wives. Let's choose joy!

◎ My Thoughts

How do I view my world? Am I focusing on what is wrong, or am I looking at what God can do? _____

_____

_____

_____

_____

♡ My Prayer

God of all creation, I praise you for your wisdom, your power, and your ability to bring joy and beauty into my world. Thank you for the mighty work you continue to do in every area of my life. I will rejoice and be glad, because you have done great things! Help me to stop worrying and fretting over circumstances. Instead, help me to keep my eyes on you and trust in your grace and power. Help me to shine your light of joy and hope, so that all may see your glorious strength in my life. In Jesus' name, amen.

This week I am praying for: _____

_____

_____

_____

_____

_____

_____

☼ My Choices

* This week I will choose to be glad and rejoice in who God is and what he can do.

* This week I will choose to stop being afraid and focusing on the negative.

* This week I will choose to live in wonder and expectancy of what God can do through my life.

* This week I will choose to: _____

_____

_____

_____

_____

◊ Couple's Discussion Starter

How is it possible for us to rejoice and not fear in difficult circumstances?

📖 For Further Reading: PSALMS 118–119

The joy that Jesus gives is the result of our
disposition being at one with his own.

—OSWALD CHAMBERS

Week 27

Pampered Wives

📖 **Key Scripture:** Amos 4:1–3

Listen to me, you "fat cows" of Samaria, you women who oppress the poor and crush the needy and who are always asking your husbands for another drink! The Sovereign LORD has sworn this by his holiness: "The time will come when you will be led away with hooks in your noses. Every last one of you will be dragged away like a fish on a hook! You will leave by going straight through the breaks in the wall; you will be thrown from your fortresses. I, the LORD, have spoken!"

The truest self-respect is not to think of self.

—HENRY WARD BEECHER

 ## Reflection

"Fat cows"? No sweet, soft message here! The prophet Amos delivered a hard word to the Israelite wives who were living with no regard for anyone but themselves. These women had grown complacent in caring for others, instead hoarding wealth and other fine things for their own gain. Strong drink was more important to them than living loving, grace-filled lives—so much so that they simply sat back and commanded their husbands to get them another drink!

This passage is both convicting and encouraging. It convicts us to repent of our self-absorbed tendencies, and it encourages us to move out of our comfort zones and step into the joy of loving God by serving others. May we never become like these selfish, self-centered, and pampered wives!

How can we be different? Let's begin by not focusing on all the things we want to satisfy our own cravings, while ignoring the needs of those who are less fortunate. Instead, let's pursue opportunities to serve and care for others in need. We can ask God to show us how and where we can best serve others by using the unique gifts and talents he has given us. There are opportunities in our own communities as well as around the world. Where is God calling you to reach out beyond yourself?

⊙ My Thoughts

Am I in danger of becoming like the women in our passage today? Am I ignoring the needs of others, while only feeding my own desires? _____

_____

_____

_____

_____

♡ My Prayer

Loving and patient Father, I praise you, for you are a holy God. You are righteous and forgiving. Thank you for meeting my needs. Oh, Lord, I want to serve you by caring for others. Convict me and show me the areas in my life where I am consumed with myself. Show me how you want me to reach out and care for those who are less fortunate. Enrich my life with a sincere and genuine love for the people in my community and around the world. In Jesus' name I pray, amen.

This week I am praying for: _____

_____

_____

_____

_____

_____

_____

☼ My Choices

* This week I will choose to see the needs of the people around me.

* This week I will choose to reach out and help others in need.

* This week I will choose to recognize and change those areas in my life where I have been greedy and self-centered.

* This week I will choose to: _____

_____

_____

_____

_____

◊ Couple's Discussion Starter

What are some practical ways we as a couple can reach out and help others in need?

📖 For Further Reading: THE BOOK OF AMOS

No indulgence of passion destroys the spiritual nature so much as respectable selfishness.

—GEORGE MACDONALD

Week 28

Pouting Prophet

📖 Key Scripture: JONAH 4:6–7, 10–11

The LORD God arranged for a leafy plant to grow there, and soon it spread its broad leaves over Jonah's head, shading him from the sun. This eased some of his discomfort, and Jonah was very grateful for the plant.

But God also prepared a worm! The next morning at dawn the worm ate through the stem of the plant so that it soon died and withered away. . . .

Then the LORD said, "You feel sorry about the plant, though you did nothing to put it there. And a plant is only, at best, short lived. But Nineveh has more than 120,000 people living in spiritual darkness, not to mention all the animals. Shouldn't I feel sorry for such a great city?"

Self-pity is our worst enemy and if we yield to it,
we can never do anything wise in this world.

—HELEN KELLER

 Reflection

Jonah didn't want to go to Nineveh to preach repentance, so he ran the other way. When he found himself in the belly of a big fish, he called out to God, and God saved him. He then obeyed God, preached to the Ninevites, and watched as they repented of their evil ways and turned to God! You would think that Jonah would have been thrilled at the success of his mission. Instead, he went away and pouted, because God didn't destroy the city. (Jonah really didn't like those Ninevites!)

Jonah was in the middle of a pity party when God used a plant to help put things in perspective. God gave Jonah a plant to shield him from the heat of the sun, then allowed the plant to quickly die. The point? Jonah was more concerned about a single plant than he was about the 120,000 men and women in Nineveh.

Perspective brings pity parties to an end. When was the last time you had a little pity party? Maybe the reason for it seems small to you now, but at the time, you probably thought you had perfect grounds for pouting. When we step back and look at the needs of others, however, our pity parties often seem petty. Putting things in an eternal perspective makes most small issues seem not worth the whining.

So why, then, do we whine and pout? Many times it is because we narrowly focus on our own little worlds and fail to see the bigger picture of what God is doing or can do through our circumstances. Sometimes we focus only on how a situation affects us and forget to think about others. Like Jonah, we could stand to broaden our perspective, see the eternal picture, and put the pouting aside!

ⓞ My Thoughts

Is there any area of my life in which I'm feeling sorry for myself? How can I begin to have a bigger, more eternal perspective? _____

_____

_____

♡ My Prayer

Sovereign God, divine Father, I praise you, because you know all and see all. You have the eternal picture in view. Your Son, Jesus, knows what it is like to suffer. May I be like Jesus, who fixed his eyes on the joy set before him, enduring the cross and suffering its shame on our behalf. Help me to live with a perspective that takes the needs of others into account. Convict me when I begin to pout, and help me to change my perspective. In Jesus' name I pray, amen.

This week I am praying for: _____

_____

_____

_____

_____

☀ My Choices

* This week I will choose to stop pouting when I don't get what I want.

* This week I will choose to see the bigger picture and think about the eternal perspective.

* This week I will choose to pray about issues in my life instead of whining about them.

* This week I will choose to: _____

_____

_____

_____

_____

◊ Couple's Discussion Starter

When was the last time each of us whined or complained about something? How could a broader perspective have changed our attitudes?

📖 For Further Reading: The book of Jonah

What poison is to food,
self-pity is to life.

—Oliver C. Wilson

Week 29

What Is Good?

📖 Key Scripture: MICAH 6:6–8

What can we bring to the LORD to make up for what we've done? Should we bow before God with offerings of yearling calves? Should we offer him thousands of rams and tens of thousands of rivers of olive oil? Would that please the LORD? Should we sacrifice our firstborn children to pay for the sins of our souls? Would that make him glad?

No, O people, the LORD has already told you what is good, and this is what he requires: to do what is right, to love mercy, and to walk humbly with your God.

Mercy in us is a sign
of our interest in God's mercy.

—THOMAS MANTON

 Reflection

What does God desire from his people? Is it sacrifices? Is it going to church every Sunday? Is it giving big sums of money to ministries? Attending three Bible studies a week? Going on mission trips? All of these things are well and good, but our passage today tells us what God desires most from us. He wants us to take three specific actions: do what is right, love mercy, and walk humbly with him.

What would these three actions look like if we applied them to our marriage relationships? When God tells us to do what is right, he is pointing us toward qualities such as honesty, faithfulness, integrity, and righteousness. Are we honest and faithful wives, or do we demean our husbands behind their backs and defiantly do things to spite them?

Loving mercy involves gracefully showing kindness and compassion. God is merciful toward us, and we ought to be merciful toward others. Sometimes, though, showing mercy in our marriages is more difficult than showing mercy in other relationships. Are we compassionate toward our husbands, or would we rather complain, nag, and tell them what they have done wrong?

Finally, God tells us to walk humbly with him. As we walk closely with God, we grow in reverence and adoration of him. We recognize that all we have comes from him, and our own arrogance and selfishness is diminished. How much more pleasant would we be as wives, if we consistently walked in humility with God and not with a haughty spirit? God's words delivered through the prophet Micah speak mightily to us as Christians, but also to us as wives, don't you agree?

⑥ My Thoughts

Am I currently walking humbly with God, or am I busy going my own way? How can I begin to walk humbly with him? _____

_____

_____

_____

♡ My Prayer

Glorious and wonderful God, I praise you for your mercy and grace toward me. I praise you because you are a holy God who is righteous and just. You are the giver of all good things. Thank you for your blessings. Thank you for my marriage. Help me to walk in righteousness and to show mercy in my marriage and in life. Convict me when I am arrogantly walking my own way and living without your guidance. Help me to reflect your love in my home. In Jesus' name, amen.

This week I am praying for: _____

_____

_____

_____

_____

☼ My Choices

* This week I will choose to recognize any unrighteous behaviors in my life and seek God's strength in turning from them.

* This week I will choose to reflect God's mercy and grace in my home.

* This week I will choose to humbly draw close to God through prayer and reading his Word.

* This week I will choose to: _____

_____

_____

_____

🍃 Couple's Discussion Starter

How can we encourage each other to follow God's commands to do what is right, love mercy, and walk humbly with him?

📖 For Further Reading: MICAH 6–7

How much better I might serve God
if I had a closer communion with Him!

—WILLIAM WILBERFORCE

Week 30

The Power to Save

📖 Key Scripture: HABAKKUK 3:1–2

This prayer was sung by the prophet Habakkuk:

I have heard all about you, LORD, and I am filled with awe by the amazing things you have done. In this time of our deep need, begin again to help us, as you did in years gone by. Show us your power to save us. And in your anger, remember your mercy.

If God should have no more mercy on us
than we have charity one to another,
what would become of us?

—THOMAS FULLER

🌼 Reflection

In our passage, the prophet Habakkuk sings a beautiful prayer to God on behalf of his people. He begins with praise, acknowledging God's amazing works. We experience great joy when we praise God for all he has done and will do. But notice that Habakkuk is praising God in the midst of his deep need. Are we willing to do the same?

I must admit that I sometimes fail to praise God in the middle of a difficult situation. When I go to God in prayer, I'm quick to move straight to my requests. Habakkuk offers us a wonderful example of how we should approach God with honor and praise before we rush into our requests.

Habakkuk continues by reminding God of times in the past when he delivered the Israelites, and Habakkuk asks for that same help once again. God doesn't grow tired of our seeking his help in times of need. In fact, he wants us to bring our needs to him continually. Jesus himself encouraged his followers to keep asking, seeking, and knocking.

Next, Habakkuk makes an interesting request of God: "In your anger, remember your mercy." Recognizing God's right to discipline Israel for straying far from him, Habakkuk nevertheless pleads for God to show his mercy. You see, Habakkuk knew the character of God. He knew that while God is righteous, he is also merciful.

As positive wives, we want to be a reflection of God's

character in our homes and marriages. That means that we, too, should remember to have mercy, even when we're angry and frustrated. We may think that our anger is justified; but just as God has shown mercy to us again and again, so we ought to extend mercy to others—including our husbands.

⑥ My Thoughts

Am I devoting time to praising God during my prayer time? Am I diligent in bringing my needs to him as well?

_____

_____

_____

♡ My Prayer

Loving and merciful God, I praise you, for you are good. With mercy and compassion, you hear my prayers and care for my needs. You alone are God, and I put my hope in you. Thank you for rescuing me, even when I don't deserve it. Thank you for showing me mercy, even when you are disciplining me. Please help me to reflect your mercy and love toward everyone in my life, especially my husband. In Jesus' name I pray, amen.

This week I am praying for: _____

_____

_____

_____

☀ My Choices

★ This week I will choose to praise God for his amazing works.

★ This week I will choose to seek God's help in my time of deep need.

★ This week I will choose to show mercy to my husband, even if I am angry.

★ This week I will choose to: _____

_____

_____

_____

_____

🖋 Couple's Discussion Starter

When we're angry with each other, do we tend to react with self-righteousness and judgment, or mercy and forgiveness?

📖 For Further Reading: HABAKKUK 3

As there is no mercy too great for God to give,
so there is no mercy too little for us to crave.

—THOMAS BROOKS

Week 31

A Father's Song

📖 Key Scripture: ZEPHANIAH 3:16–17

On that day the announcement to Jerusalem will be, "Cheer up, Zion! Don't be afraid! For the LORD your God has arrived to live among you. He is a mighty savior. He will rejoice over you with great gladness. With his love, he will calm all your fears. He will exult over you by singing a happy song."

I know of no truth in the whole Bible
that ought to come home to us with such power
and tenderness as that of the love of God.

—D. L. MOODY

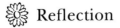 Reflection

Do you feel the love? When I read this passage, all I can do is thank the Lord for his abundant loving-kindness toward us! God is not a distant deity. He lives among us. His Spirit lives within us as believers in Christ. He is a mighty savior who has freed us from the power of sin and death through Christ's death on the cross.

Sometimes we picture God as a big, mean tyrant who shakes his fist at us and says, "I'll show you!" But here we have a description of a God who takes great delight in his people. He delights in them with gladness! Take a moment to dwell on this glad and graceful picture of God. Think about a loving parent who joyfully welcomes his child into his loving arms. Can you feel the warmth of this scene?

God's love is far beyond human love. My dear sister, see God's loving arms open wide, ready to receive you. No matter where you have been or what you have done, he invites you back to him. He wants to restore you with his love. Crawl up into his arms and feel the comfort of his embrace. Allow him to calm all your fears. Now hear his kind and gentle voice rejoicing over you with a joyful song: "I love you, dear child. You are mine, and I delight in you."

⊚ My Thoughts

Do I see God as a loving Father delighting in me, or do I see him as a mean and distant stranger? How can I keep the right perspective? _____

_____

_____

_____

_____

♡ My Prayer

Glorious and wonderful heavenly Father, your love overwhelms me. I'm amazed that you delight in me, and I praise you for the abundance of your grace-filled love. Thank you for delighting in me and rejoicing over me with joyful songs. Continue to transform me by your love. Help me to delight in you, as you delight in me. May the joy of knowing that I am completely loved by you overflow into my love for others. In Jesus' name I pray, amen.

This week I am praying for: _____

_____

_____

_____

_____

_____

_____

_____

☼ My Choices

* This week I will choose to praise God for loving me and living within me.

* This week I will choose to recognize that God delights in me.

* This week I will choose to crawl into God's arms and allow him to calm my fears.

* This week I will choose to: _____

_____

_____

_____

_____

◊ Couple's Discussion Starter

How do we picture God? How does our concept of God affect the way we feel about him?

▭ For Further Reading: PSALMS 66–68

The love of God toward you is like the Amazon River flowing down to water a single daisy.

—F. B. MEYER

Week 32

Take Courage!

📖 **Key Scripture:** HAGGAI 2:4–5

Take courage, Zerubbabel, says the LORD. Take courage, Jeshua son of Jehozadak, the high priest. Take courage, all you people still left in the land, says the LORD. Take courage and work, for I am with you, says the LORD Almighty. My Spirit remains among you, just as I promised when you came out of Egypt. So do not be afraid.

Courage is not the absence of fear;
rather, it is the ability to take action
in the face of fear.

—NANCY ANDERSON

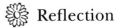 Reflection

The Israelites were about to step forward in faith. God knew their fears would get the best of them if they chose to dwell on the challenges ahead, so he sends a message filled with courage and strength. Notice that he reminds the Israelites about times in the past when he gave them victory. We, too, can be refreshed and encouraged as we reflect on the times God has brought us through difficulties. May we never forget what he has already done in our lives! When challenges come, may we hear his message of strength and hope: I am with you . . . so do not be afraid."

You may not be facing a large army in battle, but you may be facing seemingly insurmountable challenges in your marriage, your work, or with your kids. Remember, you are not alone. God is with you! Don't fret about tomorrow, but seek God's strength for today. Fear can pop into your thoughts without a moment's notice and overtake your mind, if you let it. Make a conscious effort to give your fear to God and ask for his courage, strength, and power instead. He will hold you, protect you, and give you everything you need to live in victory.

ⓖ My Thoughts

What fears tend to consume me? Am I willing to give them to God and seek his courage and strength instead? _____

_____

_____

_____

_____

_____

♡ My Prayer

Almighty God, I praise you, for you are able to do all things. Thank you for always being with me. Thank you for taking away my fears and giving me courage. Be my strength day by day, moment by moment. Guard my heart against evil. Keep me from dwelling on fears, and help me to keep my eyes on you. Thank you for being my rock and my refuge, a very present help in time of need. I love you. In Jesus' name, amen.

This week I am praying for: _____

_____

_____

_____

_____

_____

_____

_____

☀ My Choices

* This week I will choose to recognize that God is with me.

* This week I will choose to be strong in him day by day.

* This week I will choose to give my fears to him continually.

* This week I will choose to: _____

_____

_____

_____

_____

◊ Couple's Discussion Starter

Have there been fearful times in our lives when we've had to rely on God's presence and strength?

📖 For Further Reading: THE BOOK OF HAGGAI

God can secure us from fear,
either by removing the thing feared,
or by subduing the fear of the thing.

—WILLIAM BEVERIDGE

Week 33

By His Spirit

📖 **Key Scripture:** ZECHARIAH 4:6–7

Then he said to me, "This is what the LORD says to Zerubbabel: It is not by force nor by strength, but by my Spirit, says the LORD Almighty. Nothing, not even a mighty mountain, will stand in Zerubbabel's way; it will flatten out before him! Then Zerubbabel will set the final stone of the Temple in place, and the people will shout: 'May God bless it! May God bless it!'"

The greatest single distinguishing feature
of the omnipotence of God is that our imagination
gets lost when thinking about it.

—BLAISE PASCAL

By His Spirit

✤ Reflection

In our passage today, Zerubbabel was encouraged by the Lord in his responsibility to rebuild the Temple. God reminded him that the Temple would be rebuilt, not by strength or force, but by his Spirit. God wanted the Israelites to know that the victory was in his hands, not theirs.

Many times we want to forge ahead in our own strength and power when we see something that needs improvement or change. When we allow God's Spirit to do his work in the situation, however, we see mighty and miraculous results. Of course, you and I have not been given the task of rebuilding the Temple, but we do have certain responsibilities that God has given us. We can try to accomplish them with our own effort, or we can allow God's Spirit to lead us, guide us, and work through us.

The question is, will we rely on ourselves or on God? As positive wives, we must ask this question regularly—especially when it comes to our husbands. Do we try to force change or revival or spiritual leadership in them, using our own strength and force (and a little nagging), or do we look to the work of God's Spirit?

If we want to see true and lasting results, we must look to God's Spirit and not to ourselves. Instead of forcing change in our husbands, let's pray for change and ask God to do a mighty work. Let's step out of the way and stop being our husbands' personal "holy spirit." When we look to God's Spirit to do the changing, then God gets the

131

glory, and we will have the opportunity to shout with the Israelites, "May God bless it! May God bless it!"

⑥ My Thoughts

In what areas do I try to be my husband's personal "holy spirit"? How will I turn this responsibility over to the Lord?

_____

_____

_____

_____

_____

♡ My Prayer

Great and powerful God, you can do all things! I praise you for the work you do, far beyond anything I could ask or imagine. Your timing is perfect and your ways are wise. Thank you for your Holy Spirit, who works in a powerful way in our lives. Forgive me for the times I have tried to force change in my husband's life. I trust you for his spiritual growth and his walk with you. May your Spirit do a mighty work in my life and his, bringing us closer to you and to one another. In Jesus' name I pray, amen.

This week I am praying for: _____

_____

_____

_____

_____

☼ My Choices

* This week I will choose to recognize areas where I try to force change without God.

* This week I will choose to turn those areas over to God.

* This week I will choose to trust God's Spirit to do a great work in my marriage.

* This week I will choose to: _____

_____

_____

_____

_____

ᗕ Couple's Discussion Starter

Why is it better for us to ask God to do his work through his Holy Spirit, rather than trying to force something in our own might without his help?

📖 For Further Reading: ZECHARIAH 8–10

We read the Scriptures in vain if we fail to discover
that the actions of men, evil men as well as good,
are governed by the Lord God.

—ARTHUR W. PINK

Week 34

No Exclusion Clause

📖 Key Scripture: MALACHI 2:15–16

Didn't the LORD make you one with your wife? In body and spirit you are his. And what does he want? Godly children from your union. So guard yourself; remain loyal to the wife of your youth. "For I hate divorce!" says the LORD, the God of Israel. "It is as cruel as putting on a victim's bloodstained coat," says the LORD Almighty. "So guard yourself; always remain loyal to your wife."

A happy marriage is the union
of two good forgivers.

—ROBERT QUILLEN

❀ Reflection

God takes the marriage vow seriously. In Malachi's day, the Israelites did not. Divorce had become easy and commonplace—and more often than not, a glorified excuse for adultery. It was also cruel. Only men had the right to initiate divorce, and many married women found themselves suddenly unmarried, with few resources for survival.

The message of our Scripture passage is clear: God hates divorce. He wants husbands and wives to be loyal and true to their spouses. There's no exclusion clause for those who are "not happy" or those who simply don't want to "put up" with their partners anymore. Marriage is important to God! (We're not talking about cases of adultery or abuse here. Jesus speaks about adultery in Matthew 5:31–32. As for abuse, any woman experiencing abuse in her home needs to remove herself immediately and seek help.)

Our society today is a lot like Malachi's. Divorce is easy and widespread. Both Christians and non-Christians alike seem to run for divorce the moment the going gets tough. Both husbands and wives choose to follow their passions and have affairs. As positive wives, let's choose to be different!

Agree with your husband to never let the word *divorce* enter your vocabulary. Take all measures to strengthen your marriage and resolve any problems. Reflect on what you have in common and what brought you together in the first place. Ask God to help you love your husband the way *he* loves your husband. Guard your passions and save them only for your spouse.

Let's depend on God to help us build and strengthen our marriages—and show the world what the power of God can do when two people come together as one.

 My Thoughts

Do I have the mind-set of loyalty for the long haul in my marriage? Am I seeking God's strength to help me build my marriage? _____

_____

_____

♡ My Prayer

Loving and faithful God, I praise you, for your love is perfect. Thank you for your promise to never leave me or forsake me. Help me to reflect your love and loyalty in my marriage. Give me a renewed love and passion for my husband. Strengthen our marriage, and keep us loyal, faithful, and true. Do a powerful work in our lives to bond us together and protect us from distractions that could hurt that bond. Oh Lord, be glorified in our marriage! In Jesus' name I pray, amen.

This week I am praying for: _____

_____

_____

☼ My Choices

* This week I will choose to strengthen the bonds in my marriage relationship.

* This week I will choose to reflect on the blessings my husband and I have in our life together.

* This week I will choose to overlook the differences I have with my husband.

* This week I will choose to: _____

_____

_____

_____

◗ Couple's Discussion Starter

What are the strengths in our marriage relationship? What can we do to make our marriage even stronger?

📖 For Further Reading: MARK 10:1–12, EPHESIANS 5

The man and wife are partners,
like two oars in a boat.

—HENRY SMITH

Week 35

Shine!

📖 **Key Scripture:** MATTHEW 5:13–16

You are the salt of the earth. But what good is salt if it has lost its flavor? Can you make it useful again? It will be thrown out and trampled underfoot as worthless. You are the light of the world—like a city on a mountain, glowing in the night for all to see. Don't hide your light under a basket! Instead, put it on a stand and let it shine for all. In the same way, let your good deeds shine out for all to see, so that everyone will praise your heavenly Father.

My life helps to paint
my neighbor's picture of God.

—PETER HOLMES

❀ Reflection

Jesus gives us two powerful illustrations of what his followers are like: salt and light. Have you ever thought of yourself as salt and light?

Consider the qualities of salt: it preserves, it flavors, it creates thirst. As followers of Christ, we represent these same qualities to the world. We preserve the moral foundation in our society; we flavor the world with the beauty of God's wisdom, joy, and peace; and as we live for Christ, we create a thirst in others to know him. We're like salt in another way too. Just as salt loses its effectiveness when it's mixed with another substance, such as sand, so our effectiveness is diminished when we blend into the world and become conformed to its ways.

Jesus also compared us to light. As Christians, we have the responsibility of illuminating this dark world with God's love. We show the brightness of our love by our forgiveness and compassion toward others—a reflection of God's forgiveness and compassion toward us. Our light brings others to his light.

The question is, what does the world see when it looks at Christians and Christian marriages? More to the point, what does it see when it looks at *us* and *our* marriages? Does it see salt and light, or people blending into the world and living with unforgiveness and bitterness? Let's examine our influence and recognize the significance of being salt and light. May we never be guilty of losing our flavor or hiding our light under a basket.

⑥ My Thoughts

Am I allowing God to make a difference in the world through me? Are there any ways I tend to hide Christ's light? _____

_____

_____

_____

_____

♡ My Prayer

Light of the world, holy God, perfect King, I praise you for your abundant love. Thank you for giving us light to shine. Please shine the light of your love through me. Guard me from my own self-centeredness and other distractions that keep my light hidden. Allow me to flavor this world with your wisdom, joy, and peace. I want to be useful in your kingdom. In Jesus' name I pray, amen.

This week I am praying for: _____

_____

_____

_____

_____

_____

_____

☀ My Choices

* ★ This week I will choose to reflect on ways that I am salt and light in my community.

* ★ This week I will choose to recognize those areas where I tend to hide my light under a basket.

* ★ This week I will choose to be an example of Christ's love in all I do.

* ★ This week I will choose to: _____

_____

_____

_____

_____

✒ Couple's Discussion Starter

What difference would we see in this world if Christians truly shined the light of Christ's love?

📖 For Further Reading: MATTHEW 5–7

The Christian should stand out
like a sparkling diamond.

—BILLY GRAHAM

Week 36

What's in Your Heart?

📖 Key Scripture: MARK 7:20–23

It is the thought-life that defiles you. For from within, out of a person's heart, come evil thoughts, sexual immorality, theft, murder, adultery, greed, wickedness, deceit, eagerness for lustful pleasure, envy, slander, pride, and foolishness. All these vile things come from within; they are what defile you and make you unacceptable to God.

None but God knows what
an abyss of corruption is in my heart.

—ROBERT MURRAY M'CHEYNE

❀ Reflection

The Pharisees were all about outward appearances. They did things for show—to make themselves look good. They kept all the religious rules and carefully obeyed all the laws, but their hearts were full of self-righteousness, hatred, and deceit.

It's easy to point my finger at the Pharisees and say how wrong they were, until I realize how often I play the same game. Going to church, doing volunteer work, and teaching Bible studies all look so good; and don't get me wrong, they *are* good. But God doesn't look at our outward works; he looks at our hearts. It's difficult for me to know my own heart, so I must pray with the psalmist, "Create in me a clean heart, O God; and renew a right spirit within me" (Psalm 51:10 kjv). The Lord who knows my heart is able to make me new and clean. He can do the same for you.

As positive wives, let's agree to seek the Holy Spirit's conviction and help and allow him to purify our hearts so that we can be vessels who glorify God both inside and out. In the process, we are sure to recognize attitudes within our hearts that aren't so pretty. The psalmist also said, "How can a young person stay pure? By obeying your word. . . . I have hidden your word in my heart, that I might not sin against you" (Psalm 119:9–11). Filling our hearts and minds with God's Word is the key to weeding out the wickedness there. Let's commit ourselves to walking in the Word daily and memorizing Scripture passages that lead to righteousness. Then let's give all the glory to God!

⊚ My Thoughts

Do I recognize any of the traits mentioned in today's passage in my own heart? Am I willing to give these areas over to the Lord? _____

_____

_____

_____

♡ My Prayer

Powerful and perfect God, I praise you, for you are pure and holy and good. Your ways are righteous and just. Thank you for giving me your Holy Spirit to live within my heart and convict me of sin. I confess that I struggle with _____. Lord, please clean me up. I know I can't see all the ugliness in my own heart. I need your cleansing and healing from within. Make me new! In Jesus' name I pray, amen.

This week I am praying for: _____

_____

_____

_____

_____

_____

☼ My Choices

* This week I will choose to ask God to convict me of any sin that is in my heart.

* This week I will choose to fill my heart and mind with God's Word.

* This week I will choose to seek the Lord for a clean heart and ask him to do a mighty work in my life.

* This week I will choose to: _____

_____

_____

_____

_____

◊ Couple's Discussion Starter

Why does God care more about the heart than outward appearances?

📖 For Further Reading: MARK 6–7

The seeds of every wickedness lie hidden in our hearts.
They only need the convenient season to spring forth
into a mischievous vitality.

—J. C. RYLE

Week 37

A Good Return

📖 Key Scripture: LUKE 6:37–38

Stop judging others, and you will not be judged. Stop criticizing others, or it will all come back on you. If you forgive others, you will be forgiven. If you give, you will receive. Your gift will return to you in full measure, pressed down, shaken together to make room for more, and running over. Whatever measure you use in giving—large or small—it will be used to measure what is given back to you.

Kindness always brings its own reward.
The kind person will seldom be without friends.

—J. C. RYLE

 Reflection

Jesus calls us to be generous with kindness, love, and forgiveness. He also tells us to stay away from judging and criticizing others. Of course, Jesus isn't making a statement about societal laws; he is warning us not to be the type of people who are constantly pointing out the faults and shortcomings of others. If we give gracious love to others, we will receive it; if we live with a judgmental attitude, it will be returned to us as well.

So how does this speak to us as wives? Well, are we continually nit-picking and focusing on what our husbands are doing wrong, or are we encouraging and uplifting them and helping them to be the best they can be? Our passage today reminds us that we will reap what we sow. If we sow seeds of condemnation in our homes and marriages, we will reap a crop of anger, blame, and criticism directed back to us. If we plant seeds of kindness, graciousness, and love, however, we will eventually reap an overflowing reward that leads to an enriching, encouraging marriage relationship.

It's time to weed out judgment and criticism from our marriages and replace those negative attitudes with kindness and love. We are never more like Christ than when we forgive, but we are never more like the enemy, Satan, than when we accuse. May the Lord help us to be more like Jesus!

No more nit-picking! Instead, choose to build the love

in your home, beginning with your own attitude. Don't point the finger and say, "But he . . ." Be a positive wife. Be generous and gracious in showing kindness, forgiveness, and love to your husband—then watch for the amazing results that flow back to you.

 My Thoughts

In what areas do I tend to judge my husband? How can I begin to overlook his flaws and build him up instead of condemning him and tearing him down? _____

_____

_____

♡ My Prayer

Gracious Lord, I praise you for your loving-kindness and tender mercy toward me. I thank you that there is no condemnation for those who are in Christ Jesus. Because I know I am not condemned by you, I want to live without condemnation toward others, especially my husband. Help me to be generous with love and forgiveness, and remove my judgmental spirit. May your love flow through me to others in manifold measure! In Jesus' name, amen.

This week I am praying for: _____

_____

_____

_____

_____

☼ My Choices

★ This week I will choose to stop looking at my husband with an attitude of condemnation.

★ This week I will choose to notice my husband's strengths and be generous with encouragement and love.

★ This week I will choose to ask God's help to love others the way that he does.

★ This week I will choose to: _____

_____

_____

_____

_____

◗ Couple's Discussion Starter

What is an area in our relationship where we need to be less condemning of each other and more loving?

📖 For Further Reading: LUKE 6

Nothing causes us to so nearly resemble God
as the forgiveness of injuries.

—JOHN CHRYSOSTOM

A New Family

📖 Key Scripture: JOHN 1:10–13

Although the world was made through him, the world didn't recognize him when he came. Even in his own land and among his own people, he was not accepted. But to all who believed him and accepted him, he gave the right to become children of God. They are reborn! This is not a physical birth resulting from human passion or plan—this rebirth comes from God.

The saints are God's jewels,
highly esteemed by and dear to him;
they are a royal diadem in his hand.

—MATTHEW HENRY

✿ Reflection

How glorious to think that we are a part of God's family! As believers in Christ, we have been given the right to become his children. Think about that: We are the children of the High King of heaven. We have a relationship with the almighty God!

Personally, I am in awe that the God of all creation accepts me as one of his daughters. My fellow royal sister in Christ, do you see yourself in this noble position? You are a daughter of the King, dearly loved by him. Allow that thought to fill your heart and mind. Recognize your status as one of God's beloved. He is your heavenly Father, and his love transcends the human love of even the best earthly father. Isn't it beautiful to know that you can approach his throne of grace and commune with him?

When you and I see ourselves as dearly loved daughters of the King, we are transformed. Our desire becomes to walk in a manner worthy of our Lord; as we grow closer and closer to him, we begin to reflect more and more of his traits. His love begins to shine brightly through our words and actions, and people can see that we belong to him.

As God's children, we are no longer slaves to sin and our own selfish desires. We are forgiven through Christ and freed from the power of sin and death. Now we have an eternal place in God's kingdom. May we cry out together, "Thank you, Lord, for the royal privilege of being a part of your family!"

⑥ My Thoughts

As a child of God, do I live in a way that makes the family resemblance obvious to others? _____

_____

_____

_____

♡ My Prayer

Great and wonderful Father, you deserve all praise and glory. You are the High King of heaven and the maker of all things. I praise you for your sovereignty and your great love. Thank you for allowing me to be a part of your family. Thank you for being the perfect Father. You are loving, faithful, and forgiving. Help others to see these traits in me and recognize the family resemblance. May my life be a reflection of my love for you. In Jesus' name I pray, amen.

This week I am praying for: _____

_____

_____

_____

_____

_____

A New Family

☀ My Choices

* This week I will choose to see myself as a daughter of the King.

* This week I will choose to approach God as my loving heavenly Father.

* This week I will choose to live a life that reflects his love.

* This week I will choose to: _____

_____

_____

_____

_____

✒ Couple's Discussion Starter

What difference does it make in our lives to know that we are children of God?

📖 For Further Reading: JOHN 1–3

As you come to know God as your Father, living like the Father becomes the deepest yearning of your soul.

—DR. DEBORAH NEWMAN

Week 39

Searching for Truth

📖 **Key Scripture:** ACTS 17:10–12

That very night the believers sent Paul and Silas to Berea. When they arrived there, they went to the synagogue. And the people of Berea were more open-minded than those in Thessalonica, and they listened eagerly to Paul's message. They searched the Scriptures day after day to check up on Paul and Silas, to see if they were really teaching the truth. As a result, many Jews believed, as did some of the prominent Greek women and many men.

I thirst for truth,
but shall not drink it
till I reach the source.

—ROBERT BROWNING

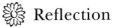 Reflection

The people of Berea were open-minded, and they searched for truth. A search for truth will always lead us to Jesus, who is the way, the truth and the life. I want to be a truth seeker too, don't you?

We definitely can't believe everything we hear. Just because someone says that something is true doesn't mean that it is. We must not be the kind of women who swallow everything people tell us, hook, line, and sinker. In today's world, there are many false teachers, just as there were in the time of the early church. People say things that sound good and tickle our ears, but their messages are not founded on God's Word.

I admire the intensity of the Bereans' search. They knew that the Scriptures are the only sure source of truth. Day after day they dug deep to find truth in the Scriptures, so they could know whether or not to believe the teachings of Paul and Silas.

When someone tells us, "God says this," or "God says that," we need to check it out in God's Word. We need to be like the Bereans and diligently search the Scriptures to determine what is true. You see, as we get to know the Bible, we become wiser. We become more discerning of false statements. Let's not be the kind of people who are content to hear a happy message. Instead, let's commit ourselves to learning God's Word and searching the

Bible to know the truth. Then let's hold on to that truth, because the truth is what sets us free.

⊚ My Thoughts

Am I a seeker of truth, or do I just accept whatever I hear?

_____

_____

_____

_____

_____

♡ My Prayer

God of all truth, I praise you because I find the truth in you. Your truth transforms me. Thank you for giving me the truth of your Word. Thank you for giving me wisdom and discernment. Thank you for your Son, who is the way, the truth, and the life. Teach me more, so that I can discern when something is false. Lead me down the pathway of truth, and keep me from any false roads that lead to destruction. I love you, and I love your Word. In Jesus' name I pray, amen.

This week I am praying for: _____

_____

_____

_____

_____

_____

☼ My Choices

* This week I will choose to search the Scriptures daily to know God's truth.

* This week I will choose to love the truth and not just believe everything I hear.

* This week I will choose to ask God for wisdom and discernment.

* This week I will choose to: _____

_____

_____

_____

_____

◊ Couple's Discussion Starter

Why is it important for us to search and study the Scriptures?

📖 For Further Reading: ACTS 16–17

O faithful Christian, search the truth,
hear truth, learn truth, love truth,
speak the truth, hold the truth till death.

—JOHN HUS

Week 40

Blessed Are the Peacemakers

📖 **Key Scripture:** ROMANS 5:1–2

Since we have been made right in God's sight by faith, we have peace with God because of what Jesus Christ our Lord has done for us. Because of our faith, Christ has brought us into this place of highest privilege where we now stand, and we confidently and joyfully look forward to sharing God's glory.

There is no grace unless God bestows it,
and there is no real peace unless it flows forth
from God's reconciliation with sinful man.

—J. J. MULLER

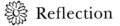 ## Reflection

Peace with God. Think about it. God went to great lengths to bring us to a place of peace with him, by offering the life of his only begotten Son. Now, through faith in Christ, sinful people are able to have peace with a holy God! To me, this is one of the most beautiful passages in all of Scripture. What blessed joy there is in knowing that while we were enemies of God, Christ chose to offer his life on the cross as a payment for our sin! Because of what he has done, we have been brought to a position of "highest privilege" and undeserved grace.

Does it amaze you, as it does me, that the God of all creation would pursue peace with us? He is the God of peace, Jesus is the Prince of Peace, and peace is a fruit of God's Holy Spirit. In the Sermon on the Mount, Jesus said, "Blessed are the peacemakers, for they will be called sons of God" (Matthew 5:9 NIV).

Since God made the ultimate sacrifice to create peace with us, are we willing to pursue peace with others, especially our husbands? Sometimes maintaining or renewing peace demands a sacrifice on our part as peacemakers. Perhaps pursuing peace requires us to give up the desire for something we want. It may mean denying ourselves something we think we deserve. Building toward peace could involve making an apology, or stepping down off our high horse in a certain area.

What are you willing to do to create peace between

you and your spouse? Certainly, peace requires something from both parties, but as much as it is up to us, we must pursue it. As we reflect on God's sacrifice for us, let's give thanks and remember that we, too, need to pursue peace with one another.

⊚ My Thoughts

What keeps me from having peace with my husband and other people? _____

_____

_____

♡ My Prayer

Glorious God of peace, I praise you, for you are the ultimate peacemaker. Thank you for pursuing peace with me. Thank you for allowing your Son to die on the cross to pay the penalty for my sin. Thank you that through faith in what Christ has done, I have peace with you. Oh Lord, I want to have peace in my marriage and in all my relationships! Show me what I need to do to pursue peace. Give me the strength and sacrificial love I need to be a peacemaker. Allow your peace to flow through me. In Jesus' name I pray, amen.

This week I am praying for: _____

_____

_____

_____

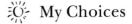 My Choices

* This week I will choose to rejoice in the fact I have peace with God through Jesus' sacrifice on the cross.

* This week I will choose to pursue peace in my marriage and in all my relationships.

* This week I will choose to be a peacemaker, even when it requires sacrifice on my part.

* This week I will choose to: _____

_____

_____

_____

_____

Couple's Discussion Starter

What sacrifices can each of us make to build peace in our relationship?

For Further Reading: ROMANS 5–8

Speak, move, act in peace,
as if you were in prayer.
In truth this is prayer.

—FRANÇOIS FENELON

Week 41

What Love
Looks Like

📖 Key Scripture: 1 CORINTHIANS 13:4–7

Love is patient and kind. Love is not jealous or boastful or proud or rude. Love does not demand its own way. Love is not irritable, and it keeps no record of when it has been wronged. It is never glad about injustice but rejoices whenever the truth wins out. Love never gives up, never loses faith, is always hopeful, and endures through every circumstance.

The point . . . is not to suggest that the world is so big that it takes a great deal of love to embrace it all, but that the world is so bad that it takes a great kind of love to love it at all.

—B. B. WARFIELD

✾ Reflection

In our passage today, Paul provides us with a power-packed definition of love. Why is it so difficult for us to maintain a 1 Corinthians 13–type of love? The fact is, we're all sinful human beings, and we tend toward selfishness and self-centeredness at times. The love Paul describes is a God-type love. God's love for us is patient and kind. It is not easily angered, and it keeps no record of wrongs. It never fails. Our God has an abundant, redeeming, grace-filled love for us that goes far beyond our human ability to love.

The fact is, the Bible doesn't just say that God loves; it says that God *is* love. His love sets the standard for us. Thankfully, he doesn't leave us fumbling to try to love others with a perfection and purity that's beyond us. We can never meet his standard in our own power. Rather, God helps us to love as he loves by the power of his Spirit within us.

Jesus said that as we abide in him and he in us, we will bear much fruit. He also said that without him we can do nothing. We're powerless to sincerely love others in our own strength, but as we ask God to pour his love through us, we can love in *his* strength. His love through us can do great things. It forgives and overlooks differences. It is patient and kind and not easily angered. It keeps no record of wrongs. Can you imagine what that kind of love can do for your marriage?

When it comes to loving others, we are weak, but he is strong. As positive wives, let's be diligent to ask God for his power to love our husbands and our families. Then let's watch what a difference his perfect love makes in all our relationships!

⑥ My Thoughts

In what areas do I need to seek God's help and strength to love my husband and those around me? _____

_____

_____

♡ My Prayer

Loving and faithful God, I praise you for your great love toward me. Your love is perfect and abundant. Thank you for your Holy Spirit living within me and for the power he gives me to love others. Increase my love for my husband and the people around me. Love boldly and boundlessly through me. I want the love I have for others to reflect your love for me. Pour yourself through me, and touch those around me for your glory. In Jesus' name I pray, amen.

This week I am praying for: _____

_____

_____

_____

_____

☼ My Choices

* This week I will choose to love my husband with a 1 Corinthians 13–type of love.

* This week I will choose to ask God to pour his divine love through me.

* This week I will choose to reflect God's love in everything I do and say.

* This week I will choose to: _____

_____

_____

_____

_____

✎ Couple's Discussion Starter

In what ways does our love for each other reflect the description of love in 1 Corinthians 13?

📖 For Further Reading: 1 CORINTHIANS 12–13

Love—and the unity it attests to—is the mark Christ gave Christians to wear before the world. Only with this mark may the world know that Christians are indeed Christians and that Jesus was sent by the Father.

—FRANCIS SCHAEFFER

Week 42

Crucified with Christ

📖 **Key Scripture:** GALATIANS 2:19–21

I have been crucified with Christ. I myself no longer live, but Christ lives in me. So I live my life in this earthly body by trusting in the Son of God, who loved me and gave himself for me. I am not one of those who treats the grace of God as meaningless. For if we could be saved by keeping the law, then there was no need for Christ to die.

Christ on the cross delivers from the penalty of sin (Prophet). Christ at God's right hand delivers from the power of sin (Priest). Christ coming in the clouds delivers from the presence of sin (King).

—D. L. MOODY

🌼 Reflection

When we place our faith in Christ, we become new creations. Old things pass away. The sinful nature that dominated our lives now gives way to a Christ-centered nature. How is this possible? Through the Cross.

The purpose of Christ's death on the cross was to pay the penalty for our sin. As Paul makes clear, we could never earn our way to heaven through good works or trying to obey the law; if that were possible, then Christ died needlessly. But because of Jesus' sacrifice on the cross, we have been freed from the power and penalty of sin. We have died to our old selves. Certainly, we still sin in our earthly bodies, but we have the wonderful assurance of God's forgiveness as well as the blessing of knowing that Christ lives in us and gives us the power and strength to live for him.

My friend, does Christ make a difference in your life? Does he make a difference in your marriage? It is one thing to simply know about Christ; it is another thing to be transformed by him by placing your life in his hands. How beautiful and positive is the woman who no longer lives with self as the center of her universe, but rather lives for Christ! May we have the same attitude that Paul had— no longer living for ourselves but living for the one who loves us and gave himself for us.

 My Thoughts

How has Christ transformed my life? Have I died to self? Am I living in him? _____

_____

_____

_____

_____

♡ My Prayer

Dear God, you are my redeemer, my savior, and my king. I was dead in sin, but you made me alive in you. Thank you for Christ's death and resurrection on my behalf. Thank you for the transforming power of the Cross. Thank you for your Spirit living in me. Please continue to change me day by day. I want to be more like you! Help me to stop living a self-centered life, and lead me to live a Christ-centered one. May your life and love flow through me to my husband and to others. In Jesus' name, amen.

This week I am praying for: _____

_____

_____

_____

_____

_____

_____

_____

My Choices

- This week I will choose to seek God's help in dying to my old self-centered ways.
- This week I will choose to ask God to do a transforming work in my life and help me live for him.
- This week I will choose to thank God for loving me and giving his Son to pay the penalty for my sin.
- This week I will choose to: ________________________

____

____

____

____

Couple's Discussion Starter

What does the cross of Christ mean to each of us, individually and as a couple?

For Further Reading: Galatians 3–5

The beginning of self-mastery is to be mastered
by Christ, to yield to his lordship.

—D. G. Kehl

God's Guarantee

📖 **Key Scripture:** EPHESIANS 1:13–14

You also have heard the truth, the Good News that God saves you. And when you believed in Christ, he identified you as his own by giving you the Holy Spirit, whom he promised long ago. The Spirit is God's guarantee that he will give us everything he promised and that he has purchased us to be his own people. This is just one more reason for us to praise our glorious God.

Assurance . . . enables a child of God to feel
that the great business of life is a settled business,
the great debt a paid debt, the great disease a healed
disease and the great work a finished work.

—J. C. RYLE

✿ Reflection

Not all guarantees can be trusted. When I see a commercial on television for a new gizmo-gadget that promises "satisfaction guaranteed"—plus, if you order now, you'll receive a free juicer and a set of steak knives— hmmm . . . I'm not so sure the company will come through. The reliability of a guarantee depends on the ones who are doing the guaranteeing; some are trustworthy and some are not.

There is one guarantee, however, in which a believer in Christ can have full assurance. It is guaranteed by the one who is faithful and true: God, the High King of heaven, creator of all things. He has given us a guarantee of salvation through faith in his Son, Jesus Christ. When you place your faith in Christ, God counts you as his very own.

Isn't that a wonderful statement? Don't you feel precious in your heavenly Father's sight, just knowing that he considers you one of his own people? But then, he didn't want to leave any doubt. And you know us; we're a doubting sort. The enemy constantly whispers in our ears, *Did God really say he would save you? Surely you're not good enough to be one of his very own.*

Whenever those little doubts come creeping in, hold on to the fact that God has given you the perfect guarantee that you are his: the Holy Spirit who lives within you. The Holy Spirit is his "guarantee" until the day of redemption. The term used in the NIV translation of this passage, "Seal," refers to the royal seal that was used by a king as a guarantee that he would keep his word. We have a heavenly King who is faithful and true and will keep his word. We may not be able to trust a television guarantee, but we can certainly trust the High King of heaven's royal guarantee, bought at the price of his Son's blood. My sister, never let doubt creep into your mind again!

⊚ My Thoughts

Do I have any doubts concerning my salvation? Am I willing to trust God's guarantee? _____

_____

♡ My Prayer

Faithful Father, I praise you, because I can trust you. I trust your unfailing love for me. I trust your plans for me. I trust that you will never leave me. Your guarantee is your Spirit, who lives within me. Thank you for the assurance that I am sealed until the day of redemption. I believe your Word is true. Thank you for sending your Son to pay the penalty for my sins. Help me to live in confidence, knowing that I am eternally loved by You. In Jesus' name I pray, amen.

This week I am praying for: _____

_____
_____
_____

☼ My Choices

* This week I will choose to trust God's guarantee.

* This week I will choose to stop dwelling on doubts.

* This week I will choose to thank God for his Holy Spirit living inside of me.

* This week I will choose to: _____

_____

_____

_____

_____

𝒲 Couple's Discussion Starter

What does it mean to us to know that through faith in Christ, we are sealed until the day of redemption?

📖 For Further Reading: EPHESIANS 1–3

Faith alone justifies, through Christ alone.
Assurance is the enjoyment of that justification.

—SINCLAIR FERGUSON

Week 44

Works in Progress

📖 Key Scripture: PHILIPPIANS 1:3–6

Every time I think of you, I give thanks to my God. I always pray for you, and I make my requests with a heart full of joy because you have been my partners in spreading the Good News about Christ from the time you first heard it until now. And I am sure that God, who began the good work within you, will continue his work until it is finally finished on that day when Christ Jesus comes back again.

Gratitude to God makes even a
temporal blessing a taste of heaven.

—WILLIAM ROMAINE

🌸 Reflection

A thankful heart erupts into great joy. You can't help but experience joy when you count your blessings. Go ahead. Try it. Take a moment right now to practice thankfulness. Begin by thanking God for who he is and what he means to you. He is your savior, your redeemer, your protector, your provider, your shepherd, and your king. Thank him for the many blessings he has showered upon you.

Next, thank him for the people in your life; pray for them, and thank God for the work he is doing in their lives. Your requests will be made with great joy as you reflect on your thankfulness for each person. Specifically thank God for your husband and the work God is doing in his life. Pray for your husband's spiritual strength. Pray with joy!

Our passage today not only shows us a beautiful and joyful way to pray for others; it also reminds us that God isn't finished with us yet. God began a good work in each of us, and he will continue his work until it is finished. And when is God's work in us finally finished? Not until the day Christ Jesus returns! We are works in progress. Our husbands are works in progress. So are our family members and friends. Not one of us is a finished product yet. Let's agree to give thanks with joy every day for the people in our lives, keeping in mind that God is continuing to do a great work in them—and in us.

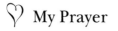 My Thoughts

Am I living with a thankful heart, or do I focus on the
negative and grumble and complain? _____

_____

_____

_____

_____

♡ My Prayer

Great protector and provider, I praise you because you
can do all things. I praise you for the mighty and wonderful plans you have for each of our lives. Thank you for
continuing to complete the good work you have started.
Thank you for the people in my life, especially my husband. Thank you for the work that you are doing in them.
Help me to remember that all of us are works in progress
in your kingdom. May the final products be for your kingdom's glory! In Jesus' name I pray, amen.

This week I am praying for: _____

_____

_____

_____

_____

_____

_____

_____

☼ My Choices

* This week I will choose to thank God continually for the people in my life.

* This week I will choose to joyfully pray for the people in my life and for the work God wants to do in them and through them.

* This week I will choose to recognize that my husband is a work in progress—and I am too.

* This week I will choose to: _____

_____
_____
_____
_____

◊ Couple's Discussion Starter

How does it help our relationship to know that we are both still works in progress?

For Further Reading: PHILIPPIANS 1–2

Gratitude is not only the greatest of virtues
but the parent of the others.

—CICERO

Week 45

Deep Roots

📖 **Key Scripture:** Colossians 2:6–7

Just as you accepted Christ Jesus as your Lord, you must continue to live in obedience to him. Let your roots grow down into him and draw up nourishment from him, so you will grow in faith, strong and vigorous in the truth you were taught. Let your lives overflow with thanksgiving for all he has done.

As the river seeks the sea, so Jesus, I seek thee!
O let me find thee and melt my life into thine forever.

—Charles H. Spurgeon

 Reflection

Recently a tree in our yard fell over. It was a fairly young tree, and its root system had not yet grown deep into the soil. When a huge gust of wind came along during a storm, it knocked the tree down. Of course, this never would have happened if the tree had developed a hardy root system. Strong roots are essential to the well-being of a tree. They're also essential for the well-being of a Christian.

Paul told the Colossians to be firmly rooted in Christ. You see, many different teachers with many different philosophies were surfacing at the time Paul wrote this letter. He knew that if the Christians in Colossae didn't grow deep in their faith and knowledge of the Lord Jesus, the trends and thinking of their culture would lead them astray. The same is true today.

How can we put down deep roots? By studying God's Word and knowing his truth. What did Jesus say? How did he live? How did he reach out and touch others in kindness and compassion? What was the purpose of his life, death, and resurrection? These are the truths that make our roots grow deep in Christ. Our roots also grow deep as we fellowship regularly with him in prayer.

Paul not only encouraged the Colossians to put down deep roots; he also told them to "draw up nourishment" from Jesus. Another Bible translation puts it this way: We need to be "rooted and built up in him" (NIV). As positive wives, we want to find our identity in Christ and not in our husbands. Jesus is a sure and secure foundation, and those who build their lives on him will not be shaken. As our roots grow deep and we build our lives on the Lord, we will overflow with thankfulness for what God has done and is doing in our lives. Strong is the wife whose roots are firmly planted in Christ!

My Thoughts

How am I growing in Christ? Do I have deep roots, or do I tend to fall over when challenges come? ______________

____

____

My Prayer

Divine Trinity, I praise you for your completeness and goodness. I praise you, because you are strong, secure, and true. Thank you for allowing me to know you. Help me to draw closer to you and allow my roots to grow deeper in you. Strengthen my spirit and help me grow strong in you. Help me to be so firmly planted in my love and faith in Christ that no false thinking can sway me and no challenge in life can move me. In Jesus' name I pray, amen.

This week I am praying for: ______________________

____

____

☀ My Choices

* This week I will choose to let my roots grow down deep in Christ by studying his Word.

* This week I will choose to examine what it means to build my life on Christ.

* This week I will choose to thank God for helping my faith grow stronger.

* This week I will choose to: _____

_____

_____

_____

_____

✒ Couple's Discussion Starter

How can we grow our roots down deep in Christ and build our life on him as a couple?

📖 For Further Reading: Colossians 1–2

Jesus Christ is the centre of everything and the object of everything, and he who does not know Him knows nothing of the order of nature and nothing of himself.

—Blaise Pascal

Pleasing God, Not People

📖 Key Scripture: 1 THESSALONIANS 2:3–4

You can see that we were not preaching with any deceit or impure purposes or trickery.

For we speak as messengers who have been approved by God to be entrusted with the Good News. Our purpose is to please God, not people. He is the one who examines the motives of our hearts.

God and his truth cannot be changed;
the gospel is not negotiable.

—JOHN MARSHALL

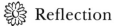 Reflection

Are you a people pleaser? Generally speaking, we all enjoy having people like us. But pleasing others can't be our first priority. Paul stated that his purpose was not to please people, but to please God. When it came to sharing God's message, Paul had a choice. He could preach what people wanted to hear and make them like him, or he could preach the pure gospel message and risk being rejected.

What is the pure gospel? We are all sinners and have fallen short of God's glory, but the free gift of God is eternal life through Jesus Christ. In our world today, this gospel is offensive to those who follow the "whatever works for you" philosophy of religion. As a result, many of us shy away from proclaiming the full gospel out of fear of what people will think of us.

Paul knew that he must answer to God for what he said, so he preached the pure gospel and not what was popular at the time. Paul also knew that he couldn't hide anything from God, because God looks at the heart. We, too, must account to God for what we say, and we must examine our motives as we share the gospel with others. Recognizing that God knows the motives of our hearts keeps us humble. It keeps us on our knees, praying, "Lord, help me to shine your light with pure motives and a clean heart."

Is there ever a time when our motives are 100 percent pure? Unfortunately our selfish tendencies often seep in, even when we're sharing the gospel. But God can use even our selfish motives for his work. Let us continually seek his help to have pure motives in all that we do and say and trust that God can take whatever we offer and use it for eternal purposes. Let's be God pleasers, not people pleasers!

⊚ My Thoughts

Am I more concerned about pleasing God or pleasing people, especially when it comes to sharing the gospel message? _____

_____

♡ My Prayer

Beautiful Savior, I praise you for reaching down and saving a sinner like me. Thank you for the sacrifice of Jesus on the cross. Thank you that he rose again, giving us the promise of eternal life. Thank you for allowing me to be a recipient of your grace. Help me to love like Jesus loves. Help me to be filled with grace toward others, because of the grace you've shown to me. May my motives be pure, and may my life shine forth with the beauty of your salvation! I love you, Lord, and I want to please you above all others. In Jesus' name, amen.

This week I am praying for: _____

_____

_____

☀ My Choices

* This week I will choose to examine the Scriptures to know the pure gospel message.

* This week I will choose to pray for pure motives when sharing God's truth.

* This week I will choose to look for opportunities to tell someone the Good News of Jesus Christ.

* This week I will choose to: _____

_____

_____

_____

_____

◊ Couple's Discussion Starter

How can we recognize when someone is preaching just to please people, not God?

📖 For Further Reading: 1 THESSALONIANS 1–3

The gospel will never be fashionable at any
period of history or in any country.

—JULES-MARCEL NICOLE

Week 47

Foolish Fights

📖 Key Scripture: 2 TIMOTHY 2:23–26

*Again I say, don't get involved in foolish, ignorant argu-
ments that only start fights. The Lord's servants must
not quarrel but must be kind to everyone. They must be
able to teach effectively and be patient with difficult people. They should gently teach those who oppose the truth.
Perhaps God will change those people's hearts, and they
will believe the truth. Then they will come to their senses
and escape from the Devil's trap. For they have been held
captive by him to do whatever he wants.*

People are usually more convinced
by reasons they discovered themselves
than by those found by others.

—BLAISE PASCAL

 Reflection

From finances to dirty socks to toothpaste tubes, couples rarely have trouble finding something to argue about. It's almost humorous to think back to some of the petty things that have been the center of many of our foolish fights. In today's passage Paul tells us to not get involved in silly disputes. We would be wise to heed these words in our marriages and recognize that some things just aren't worth the argument. There are also times when we can agree to disagree with our husbands on certain points. Every little annoyance doesn't have to become an issue. As positive wives, we need to be discerning about when to overlook an affront and when to make it a point of discussion.

Paul also reminds us to be patient with difficult people. All of us have difficult people in our lives. We may never see eye to eye with them, but we can be patient with them and allow the Lord to do his work in their lives.

Remember, God can do a better job of changing people's hearts by his Spirit than we can by trying to force a position or argue a point. We can gently and patiently share truth, but then let's pray and trust God to change people's hearts. We will make a positive impact on the people around us—especially our husbands—if we speak the truth in love and avoid unnecessary arguments. Let's determine to argue less, pray more, and stop sweating the silly small stuff!

⊚ My Thoughts

Am I getting annoyed with my husband over things that don't matter? In what areas do I need to be more patient and overlook affronts? _____

_____

_____

_____

_____

♡ My Prayer

Patient and gentle Father, I praise you for your mercy and forgiveness toward me. I praise you for your kindness and understanding. Thank you for your Holy Spirit, who helps me to be patient and discerning. Keep me from getting worked up over things that don't matter, especially in my marriage. Help me share the truth in love and be patient with difficult people. Give me the ability to deal with others in genuine love. In Jesus' name I pray, amen.

This week I am praying for: _____

_____

_____

_____

_____

_____

_____

_____

☼ My Choices

* This week I will choose to overlook petty differences and small annoyances.

* This week I will choose to pray for patience with the difficult people in my life.

* This week I will choose to speak the truth in love and trust God to change people's hearts.

* This week I will choose to: _____

_____

_____

_____

_____

◊ Couple's Discussion Starter

How can we improve the way we argue? What can we learn from Paul's advice?

📖 For Further Reading: THE BOOK OF 2 TIMOTHY

There's only one thing worse than the man
who will argue over anything, and that's the man
who will argue over nothing.

—EDWARD GIBBON

Right Teaching, Right Living

📖 Key Scripture: Titus 2:1–3

As for you, promote the kind of living that reflects right teaching. Teach the older men to exercise self-control, to be worthy of respect, and to live wisely. They must have strong faith and be filled with love and patience.

Similarly, teach the older women to live in a way that is appropriate for someone serving the Lord. They must not go around speaking evil of others and must not be heavy drinkers. Instead, they should teach others what is good.

So let our lips and lives
Express the holy gospel we profess;
So let our works and virtues shine
to prove the doctrine all divine.

—Isaac Watts

 ## Reflection

I want to "promote the kind of living that reflects right teaching," don't you? In order to reflect right teaching, however, we must receive it. There are many ways we receive right teaching, including studying the Bible on our own, going to a regular Bible study or Sunday-school class, and attending a weekly church service that offers solid Bible teaching. The key is to make sure that the teaching we receive is wholesome, true, and purely from God's Word, rather than from man's perspective.

Memorizing Scripture passages can help us reflect God's truth in our daily lives. Here's an idea: choose a passage that challenges or inspires you and write it on an index card. Keep the card with you so you can reflect on the scripture throughout the week. Soon you will discover that the more you have God's Word in your mind and heart, the more it will play out in your words and actions.

Our passage today encourages us to live as followers of Christ. Paul identifies two ways to do this (although there are many others): don't slander other people, and don't be heavy drinkers. Maligning another person says a great deal about the character of the one doing the maligning. Slander and gossip aren't simply mouth issues; they're heart issues. Heavy drinking shows that a person is depending on alcohol rather than finding her sufficiency in God. It can also lead to other sins, so Paul wisely instructs women to guard against drinking too much.

It's only as our lives begin to reflect character, self-control, and godliness that we earn the right and privilege to teach others what is good. Let's guard our hearts and mouths in order to build up—not tear down—the people in our lives, and let's learn to live each day in a way that honors God. And may the Lord use each of us to further his kingdom as we reflect the truths of his Word!

⊚ My Thoughts

How does my life reflect godly living? Are there some areas where God is convicting me of the need to change?

_____

_____

♡ My Prayer

Good and perfect God, you deserve all honor and praise. You are righteous and faithful. Thank you for your Word, which teaches me how to live. Thank you for your Holy Spirit, who convicts me of sin and leads me into righteousness. I confess that I struggle with _____

_____. Guard my lips from slandering others, and lead me away from the temptation of heavy drinking. May my mouth and my life be used to glorify you and teach others what is good. In Jesus' name I pray, amen.

This week I am praying for: _____

_____

_____

☼ My Choices

* This week I will choose to learn and grow in God's Word.

* This week I will choose to memorize a verse of Scripture that will help me live with godliness.

* This week I will choose to recognize and turn from areas in my life that don't honor God.

* This week I will choose to: _____

_____

_____

◗ Couple's Discussion Starter

As a couple, are we promoting the kind of living that reflects wholesome teaching?

📖 For Further Reading: THE BOOK OF TITUS

O Lord, grant that I may do thy will as if it were my will;
so that thou mayest do my will as if it were thy will.

—ST. AUGUSTINE

Week 49

Hold On to Hope!

📖 Key Scripture: HEBREWS 10:21–25

Since we have a great High Priest who rules over God's people, let us go right into the presence of God, with true hearts fully trusting him. For our evil consciences have been sprinkled with Christ's blood to make us clean, and our bodies have been washed with pure water.

Without wavering, let us hold tightly to the hope we say we have, for God can be trusted to keep his promise. Think of ways to encourage one another to outbursts of love and good deeds. And let us not neglect our meeting together, as some people do, but encourage and warn each another, especially now that the day of his coming back again is drawing near.

If we would venture more upon
the naked promise of God, we should enter a world
of wonders to which as yet we are strangers.

—CHARLES H. SPURGEON

🌼 Reflection

Oh, what a glorious privilege we have as believers in Christ! We have the joy of knowing that we can approach God with our requests. If not for Christ's death on the cross, the guilt of our sin would keep us from approaching God's holy throne. But we are clean. Sprinkled by the blood of our wonderful Savior, we are free to draw near to him.

If you were invited to the White House to visit with the president, you would most likely go. If you were invited to visit the queen of England at Buckingham Palace, you would probably take up the invitation. We have been invited to the throne of the High King of heaven! Let us humbly, gratefully, and continually go there. We are not hopeless women, for we have access to the King of kings and Lord of lords!

My friend, place your hope in God. Hold tightly to the hope that he can do things in your life far beyond anything you could ever ask or imagine. God is trustworthy and faithful!

If you and I will hold tightly to our hope in God, we won't keep grabbing hold of our husbands, trying to find all our answers in them. Our husbands can't solve all our problems or meet all our needs. Only God can. Let's take our requests to him and find our help and comfort at his throne. The joy we'll experience as a result will overflow in encouragement to others. May our confidence in God free us from worry and guilt, and may it motivate us to inspire others to love and good deeds!

⊙ My Thoughts

What keeps me from going to God with my needs? How can I hold more tightly to the hope I have in him? _____

_____

_____

_____

_____

♡ My Prayer

God of hope, I praise you, for you are the King of kings and Lord of lords. You bring joy and strength to my weary soul. Thank you for allowing me to have access to your presence through the shed blood of Christ. What great hope I have in you! Help me to hold tightly to that hope instead of trying to find my hope and satisfaction in people. May my hope and faith in you be an encouragement to the people around me. In Jesus' name, amen.

This week I am praying for: _____

_____

_____

_____

_____

_____

_____

☼ My Choices

* This week I will choose to hope in God instead of placing my hope in my husband or other people.

* This week I will choose to enjoy the blessing and privilege of bringing my needs before the throne of grace.

* This week I will choose to think of ways to motivate others to acts of love and good works.

* This week I will choose to: _____

_____

_____

_____

_____

◗ Couple's Discussion Starter

How can we motivate each other to acts of love and good works?

📖 For Further Reading: HEBREWS 10–12

Every time we pray, our horizon is altered, our attitude to things is altered, not sometimes but every time, and the amazing thing is that we don't pray more.

—OSWALD CHAMBERS

Week 50

Planting
Seeds of Peace

📖 Key Scripture: JAMES 3:17–18

*The wisdom that comes from heaven is first of all pure. It
is also peace loving, gentle at all times, and willing to
yield to others. It is full of mercy and good deeds. It shows
no partiality and is always sincere. And those who are
peacemakers will plant seeds of peace and reap a harvest
of goodness.*

Nearly all the wisdom we possess, that is to say,
true and sound wisdom, consists of two parts:
the knowledge of God and of ourselves.

—JOHN CALVIN

🌼 Reflection

What does a woman of wisdom look like? Our passage in James gives us a beautiful description of the qualities of godly wisdom. A wise woman is, first of all, someone who leads a pure life; she is a person of moral and spiritual integrity. Secondly, she is peace loving. This in not a reference to inner peace, but rather to peace between people and peace between God and man. A know-it-all often tries to stir up an argument or dissension just to show how smart she is, but a wise woman builds bridges of peace while holding tightly to the truth.

The next trait, "gentle at all times," doesn't mean being a doormat. It means being a woman who handles herself in a kind and thoughtful way when dealing with others. Think of Jesus, who was lovingly gentle, yet firm in his message of truth. The opposite would be someone who is brash, angry, and rude, continually demanding her own way—which leads us to the next trait: "willing to yield to others." A wise woman is willing to be flexible and defer to another person's point of view. She doesn't have to be right all the time. Wisdom humbly says, "I don't know it all, and I am willing to work this out reasonably."

A wise woman is also characterized by mercy and good deeds. She is not wrapped up in her own little world but reaches out and touches others with compassion. She is sincere and genuine, and she doesn't play favorites. Finally, a wise woman is someone who plants seeds of peace with her words and actions, reaping a harvest of goodness as a result, rather than someone who plants seeds of bitterness and anger, reaping a crop of conflict.

Are you a wise woman? Read back through this reflection and think about the qualities of wisdom in the context of your marriage. Ask God to help you reflect true, godly wisdom in your home.

⑥ My Thoughts

Am I a woman of wisdom, according to this passage? What areas do I need to prayerfully work on in my personal life?

_____

_____

♡ My Prayer

God of all wisdom, I praise you, for you know all things. Your wisdom is pure, peace loving, kind, and merciful. Oh Lord, grant me a portion of your heavenly wisdom! Make me a woman of wisdom in all that I say and do. Help me to live with wisdom and gentleness, so that I can bless my husband and the people around me. Help me to be a wise wife, planting seeds of peace in my marriage. In Jesus' name I pray, amen.

This week I am praying for: _____

_____

_____

_____

☀ My Choices

* This week I will choose to ask God to develop the qualities of wisdom in me, beginning with purity.

* This week I will choose to be gentle and peace loving in my interactions with my husband and with others.

* This week I will choose to actively look for ways to show mercy and do good deeds.

* This week I will choose to: _____

_____

_____

_____

◗ Couple's Discussion Starter

In what ways do we demonstrate godly wisdom in our marriage?

📖 For Further Reading: JAMES 1–3

Holiness is a Christian's ornament,
and loving peace is the ornament of holiness.

—THOMAS MANTON

Week 51

Reality Show

📖 Key Scripture: 1 JOHN 3:18–20

Dear children, let us stop just saying we love each other; let us really show it by our actions. It is by our actions that we know we are living in the truth, so we will be confident when we stand before the Lord, even if our hearts condemn us. For God is greater than our hearts, and he knows everything.

I have found the paradox that if
I love until it hurts, then there is no hurt,
but only more love.

—MOTHER TERESA

 **Reflection**

It's easy to say we love our husbands; it's another thing to actually demonstrate it. What would it look like if we showed our husbands we loved them through our actions and not just our words? Love for a spouse is shown through a smile, a listening ear, a respectful tone of voice. It is demonstrated through a favorite meal, a back rub, or a happy greeting at the door when he comes home from work. It is seen in a sacrificial act, a denying of self, or simply saying, "I'm sorry."

The actions of love don't always come naturally. True love requires strength, determination, and selflessness. Perhaps you are thinking, *But my husband doesn't show me this kind of love.* As a positive wife, you can choose to be the one to initiate acts of love and kindness. Plant the seeds and see what grows. Most likely, loving-kindness will be returned to you.

Maybe you've come to the point where you don't feel love for your husband anymore, and you think such actions would be insincere. There is a general principle in life that says, "Actions first, feelings follow." Do the actions of love, and the feelings of love will grow. Let's determine to love our husbands, not just in words, but in deeds and in truth.

ⓖ My Thoughts

How do I demonstrate sincere love for my husband through my actions? _____

_____
_____
_____
_____
_____

♡ My Prayer

God of Love, I praise you for your unfailing love for your children. You demonstrated your love by sacrificially sending your Son to die for us. Thank you for your constant love in action. Grant to me an ounce of your pure love, so that I may sincerely love those around me. Help me to love my husband and show it through my actions. Lead me to be more loving and less condemning. Pour your loving Spirit through me. In Jesus' name I pray, amen.

This week I am praying for: _____

_____
_____
_____
_____
_____
_____
_____

☀ My Choices

* This week I will choose to do the actions of love.

* This week I will choose to guard against unloving words and actions.

* This week I will choose to ask God to give me a genuine love for my husband and for those around me.

* This week I will choose to: _____

_____

_____

_____

_____

◊ Couple's Discussion Starter

What specific actions make us feel most loved by each other?

📖 For Further Reading: THE BOOK OF 1 JOHN

Love is never lost. If not reciprocated,
it will flow back and soften and purify the heart.

—WASHINGTON IRVING

Week 52

The
Glorious Wedding

📖 Key Scripture: Revelation 19:6–8

I heard again what sounded like the shout of a huge crowd, or the roar of mighty ocean waves, or the crash of loud thunder: "Hallelujah! For the Lord our God, the Almighty, reigns. Let us be glad and rejoice and honor him. For the time has come for the wedding feast of the Lamb, and his bride has prepared herself. She is permitted to wear the finest white linen." (Fine linen represents the good deeds done by the people of God.)

There is a land of pure delight,
Where saints immortal reign;
Infinite day excludes the night,
And pleasures banish pain.

—ISAAC WATTS

 Reflection

We're going to have the perfect wedding! The "wedding feast of the Lamb" will be that glorious day when Jesus is united with his bride. Who is his bride? The followers of Christ! In a beautiful picture of true love, Jesus laid down his life on our behalf, so that we could be made pure and holy in his sight. It's the greatest love story ever told, and it's been playing out since God created Adam. One day we will be made new. We will put on our wedding clothes of fine white linen, representing the good deeds of God's people, and we will be united with our Bridegroom, Jesus, forever.

Are you looking forward with anticipation to that wonderful day? When we set our minds on that perfect wedding and our new home in heaven, we get a new perspective on our circumstances here on earth. As the old and dearly loved hymn by Helen H. Lemmel reminds us, "Turn your eyes upon Jesus. Look full in his wonderful face. And the things of earth will grow strangely dim, in the light of His glory and grace."

Oh my dear sister, picture the day when you will be standing face to face with Jesus—no more tears, no more sorrows. There is a better life coming! Don't be consumed by worries and fears over the issues and problems of this world; rather, live with hope and anticipation, knowing that your new home in eternity awaits you. Let's enjoy our lives today in light of that glorious day when we, as Christ's bride, are united with our Bridegroom!

⊚ My Thoughts

How do I find the balance between keeping my mind on eternity and living life each day in this world? _____

_____

_____

_____

_____

♡ My Prayer

Loving and wonderful heavenly Father, I look forward to that day when those of us who are believers will be joined with Jesus at the wedding feast of the Lamb. Thank you for allowing me to be a part of your divine love story. Help me to keep my eyes looking toward heaven in anticipation of that day. Keep me from living only for this world. Show me how to live here, while keeping my focus there. Thank you for the Bridegroom, my glorious Savior. I look forward to the perfect wedding and the home in heaven that awaits me. In Jesus' name I pray, amen.

This week I am praying for: _____

_____

_____

_____

_____

☼ My Choices

* This week I will choose to look forward to that glorious day when I will see Jesus face to face.

* This week I will choose to consider ways I can lay up treasure in heaven.

* This week I will choose to thank God for including me in the most wonderful love story of all time.

* This week I will choose to: _____

_____

_____

_____

_____

◊ Couple's Discussion Starter

What do we look forward to most when we think about heaven?

📖 For Further Reading: REVELATION 21–22

*The Lamb's wedding is a time for boundless pleasure,
and tears would be out of place.*

—CHARLES H. SPURGEON

Never Underestimate the
Power
of a Positive
Woman!

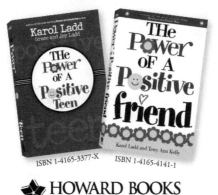

ISBN 1-4165-4143-8

An Interactive Group Study
for Positive MOMS

Designed for a dynamic, interactive group study, these eight sessions will bring the power of a positive influence into the life of every woman who attends:

1. The Portrait of a Positive Mom
2. The Power of Encouragement
3. The Power of Prayer
4. The Power of a Good Attitude
5. The Power of Strong Relationships
6. The Power of Your Example
7. The Power of Strong Moral Standards
8. The Power of Love and Forgiveness

This easy-to-use DVD has been carefully designed so that anyone can facilitate a dynamic group session. No leadership training is needed.

The Power of a Positive Mom book complements the sessions on this DVD and is available wherever good books are sold.

www.howardpublishing.com

HOWARD BOOKS
A DIVISION OF SIMON & SCHUSTER

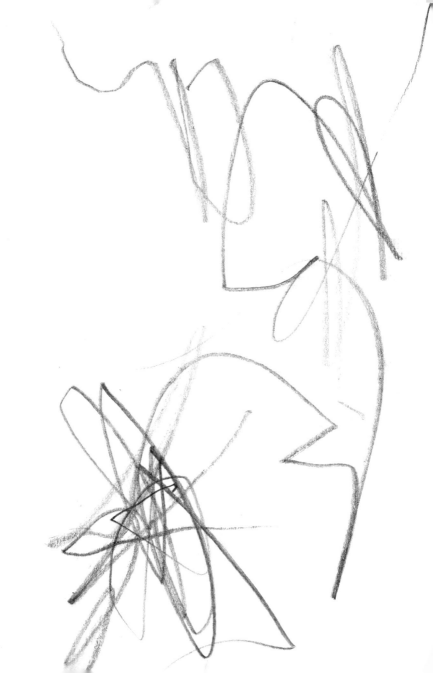